BEHAVIOR MANAGEMENT
IN TODAY'S SCHOOLS

BEHAVIOR MANAGEMENT IN TODAY'S SCHOOLS

Successful and Positive Tools for Teachers

Edward Cancio, Mary Camp, and Beverley H. Johns

ROWMAN & LITTLEFIELD
Lanham • Boulder • New York • London

Published by Rowman & Littlefield
An imprint of The Rowman & Littlefield Publishing Group, Inc.
4501 Forbes Boulevard, Suite 200, Lanham, Maryland 20706
www.rowman.com

6 Tinworth Street, London SE11 5AL

British Library Cataloguing in Publication Information Available

Library of Congress Cataloging-in-Publication Data Available

ISBN: 978-1-4758-4451-1 (cloth : alk. paper)
ISBN: 978-1-4758-4452-8 (pbk. : alk. paper)
ISBN: 978-1-4758-4453-5 (electronic)

♾ ™ The paper used in this publication meets the minimum requirements of American National Standard for Information Sciences—Permanence of Paper for Printed Library Materials, ANSI/NISO Z39.48-1992.

Printed in the United States of America

This book is dedicated to all the educators in 2018 who have given their lives or risked their lives protecting their students from harm.

Every day teachers enter their classrooms as life savers for their students. We applaud the teaching profession and all those who have chosen to make a difference in the lives of their students. The touch of a teacher is far-reaching and the smallest kind actions that teachers take every single day have a profound influence on our society.

CONTENTS

INTRODUCTION

Children enter our school doors today with many diverse needs: mental health problems, ADHD, anxiety, physical or sexual abuse, homelessness, or facing some other type of trauma. Those needs are at the forefront of education. Our society learned of several tragic shootings in schools as we were writing these two volumes on the topic of behavior management in today's schools.

There is an increasing population of students coming into our schools everyday with challenging behaviors. There are more students with autism that are exhibiting challenging behaviors. Children who have comorbid conditions such as learning disabilities, depression, autism, obsessive compulsive disorders, and traumatic brain injury with accompanying behavioral problems, are challenging the teachers. More than one quarter of children between the ages of zero to five who have entered the child welfare system exhibit trauma symptoms.

In 2011, 3.4 million referrals alleging child abuse were made to the child welfare system (Fusco and Cahalane, 2014). In a study conducted with formerly homeless mothers and their children, kindergarten to second grade, who were living in a supportive housing community, it was found that the children were at risk for externalizing behavior problems, internalizing behavior problems, and school problems. There is a relationship between adversity in the family and conduct problems (Lee et al., 2010).

Increasingly, populations of students are entering schools with psychiatric conditions such as bi-polar disorder, depression, obsessive compulsive self-destructive behaviors, and others. Teachers are struggling to understand their conditions and to provide a supportive and nurturing environment while meeting the challenge of maintaining a safe setting for their students.

Children with challenging behaviors, whether they are internalizing or externalizing, are served in today's schools in a variety of settings, from general education classes with consultation to residential treatment centers. In whatever setting, teachers must know how to assess the needs of the children, build positive relationships with them, and provide a structured environment that focuses on their academic, social, emotional, and behavioral needs. The teachers who serve these children need a comprehensive set of tools to meet their needs.

This book is volume 1 of a two-volume resource for all educators. This first volume focuses on setting the stage for effective behavior management. The second volume focuses on specific interventions.

Included in this volume are explanations of the needs of children who are coming through our school doors. This volume also focuses on the importance of evaluating the students and the necessary components to assess learning and behavior of our students. How to set up a classroom to meet the challenges faced by students in today's schools is the topic in chapter 3.

Our students need competent and caring educators who can welcome them into the classroom and chapter 4 focuses on the importance of building positive relationships with students. We focus on the quality of care that educators must exhibit when working with students who may have failed with other educators and in other schools.

Educators cannot afford to work in isolation. They must elicit the support of parents, colleagues, and other agencies to be effective. Chapter 5 focuses on the importance of collaboration.

Finally, to meet the needs of students with emotional/behavioral challenges, educators must take care of themselves before they can take care of others.

All of these topics in this first volume set the stage for making a positive difference in the lives of students.

REFERENCES

Fusco, R. and Cahalane, H. (2014). Young children in the child welfare system: What factors contribute to trauma symptomology? *Child Welfare, 92(5)*, 37–58.

Lee, S., August, G., Gewirtz, A., Klimes-Dougan, B., Bloomquist, M., and Realmuto, G. (2010). Identifying unmet mental health needs in children of formerly homeless mothers living in a supportive housing community sector of care. *Abnormal Child Psychology, 38*, 421–32.

I

WHO IS IN OUR CLASSROOMS TODAY?

Justin was born three months premature as the first child in a middle-class family. At the age of two, the parents notice that Justin has great difficulty attending to any tasks except for a few seconds. They also note that he is quick to anger and when he is upset he screams and tantrums as long as two hours. They seek an evaluation for him from the school and by a private psychologist when he is three. His parents are conscientious and receive services for Justin through early intervention for the first three years of his life. At three he is diagnosed with ADHD and emotional disturbance and the family participates in behavioral therapy. He makes some progress and is enrolled in an early childhood program where the teacher voices concern that he tantrums in class when other students attempt to interact with him. School staff meets with the parents since these behavior problems have continued for two months. The family wants to work together with the school personnel to improve Justin's behavior.

Trevor is a sixth-grade student who is very withdrawn and seems to be depressed. He is being provided special education services in a resource setting for two periods a day. Both the special education teacher and the classroom teacher voice concerns to Trevor's adoptive parents. They also have seen changes in Trevor's behavior since his birth mother made herself known to Trevor. Trevor was adopted at the age of three and prior to that time had been physically abused by his mother and was malnourished. His birth mother was an admitted drug addict and has since been drug-free for the last two years. Everyone is concerned about the impact of Trevor's mother into his life again, yet the adoptive parents don't want to deny him the opportunity to know his birth mother.

Brendan is a high school student who is exhibiting swings in his behavior. When he is on medication, he is making straight As on tests and class work. Recently he has refused to take his medication and his grades have quickly deteriorated and his behavior is of grave concern. He is becoming easily angered by his peers and has gotten into at least three physical fights precipitated by him within the last week. School staff is not sure how to handle this situation. They call Brendan and his parents in for a conference to discuss options.

Do these students fit the definition of emotional disturbance? Read on to learn more about the diversity of emotional/behavioral problems in today's classroom.

CEC INITIAL LEVEL SPECIAL EDUCATOR PREPARATION STANDARDS

CEC Initial Preparation Standard 1: Learner Development and Individual Learning Differences

1.0 Beginning special education professionals understand how exceptionalities may interact with development and learning and use this knowledge to provide meaningful and challenging learning experiences for individuals with exceptionalities.
1.1 Beginning special education professionals understand how language, culture, and family background influence the learning of individuals with exceptionalities.
1.2 Beginning special education professionals use understanding of development and individual differences to respond to the needs of individuals with exceptionalities.

CHAPTER OBJECTIVES

Readers will:

1. Define comorbidity.

2. Provide three examples of comorbidity.
3. Describe the differences between internalizing behaviors and externalizing behaviors.
4. Describe the factors that contribute to the demonstration of challenging behaviors.
5. Define the characteristics of emotional disturbance.

KEY VOCABULARY TERMS

Comorbidity—Two or more disabilities or types of mental health disorders that exist within the student.

Externalizing Behaviors—Those observable behaviors including physical and verbal aggression, classroom disruptions, and off-task behaviors.

Internalizing Behaviors—Those behaviors that are internal to the student including depression, anxiety, social withdrawal, and somatic problems.

DEFINITION AND FEDERAL ELIGIBILITY OF STUDENTS

We have an increasing population of students with emotional/behavioral problems. Children come into our classrooms with depression, oppositional defiant disorder, bi-polar disorder, anxiety disorder, and more. Will all of those students be eligible for special education services?

Let's look at the definition of emotional disturbance according to IDEA 2004, Section 504 of the Rehabilitation Act of 1973, and the Diagnostic and Statistical Manual (DSM-5).

When schools determine eligibility for special education, they utilize the definition found in the Individuals with Disabilities Education Act 2004 (IDEA 2004). That definition is as follows:

Emotional disturbance means a condition exhibiting one or more of the following characteristics over a long period of time and to a marked degree that adversely affects a child's educational performance:

a. An inability to learn that cannot be explained by intellectual, sensory, or health factors.

b. An inability to build or maintain satisfactory interpersonal relationships with peers and teachers.

c. Inappropriate types of behavior or feelings under normal circumstances.

d. A general pervasive mood of unhappiness or depression.

e. A tendency to develop physical symptoms or fears associated with personal or school problems.

Emotional disturbance includes schizophrenia. The term does not apply to children who are socially maladjusted unless it is determined that they have an emotional disturbance (34 CFR 300.8).

For an individual to be eligible for the protections under Section 504 of the Rehabilitation Act of 1973, an individual must have a physical or mental impairment that substantially limits at least one major life activity. Examples of major life activities are walking, seeing, hearing, speaking, breathing, reading, writing, performing math calculations, working, caring for oneself, performing manual tasks, and other activities.

The *Diagnostic and Statistical Manual-5* is the guide utilized by clinical psychologists and psychiatrists and other medical doctors to diagnose students with a variety of behavioral or emotional conditions. The definition that they use in general for a mental disorder is: "a syndrome characterized by clinically significant disturbance in an individual's condition, emotion regulation, or behavior that reflects a dysfunction in the psychological, biological, or developmental processes underlying mental functioning" (The Pocket Guide to the DSM-5 Diagnostic Exam, pp. 8–9). The diagnostic manual distinguishes a mental disorder from "an expectable or culturally approved response to a common stressor or loss, such as the death of a loved one" (The Pocket Guide to the DSM-5 Diagnostic Exam, p. 9). There are criteria for autism spectrum disorders, attention-deficit/hyperactivity disorders, schizophrenia spectrum and other psychotic disorders, bipolar and related disorders, depressive disorders, anxiety disorders, obsessive-compulsive and related disorders, trauma- and stressor-related disorders, dissociative disorders, somatic symptoms and related disorders, feeding and eating disorders such as anorexia nervosa, elimination disorders, sleep-wake disorders, disruptive, impulse-control, and conduct disorders, neurocognitive disorders, and personality disorders.

While educators do not provide these diagnoses, they may work with students who have received an independent evaluation and therefore received a specific diagnosis. It will be up to the educational system to determine whether the child exhibits an adverse effect on educational performance and thus qualifies as a child with a disability under the definition provided within IDEA 2004 for emotional disturbance. If the student does not have a disability that adversely impacts educational performance, the student may have been diagnosed with a specific disability under the DSM-5 and may be entitled to a Section 504 accommodation plan.

Given this information, think about whether Justin, Trevor, and Brendan have a disability under IDEA 2004.

For students from diverse backgrounds, there are a number of factors that can contribute to the demonstration of challenging behaviors that are not related to having an emotional/behavioral disorder. Therefore, in determining if a student is impacted by a disability, educators must understand the background of the students they serve. Social perceptions based on culture and the effects of poverty can be causative factors for the demonstration of challenging behaviors (Moreno, Wong-Lo, Short, and Bullock, 2014). Educators must be very cautious that they are not biased in their work with students who are diverse and exhibit behavioral challenges. It has been found that African American students were significantly under-represented in receiving assistive measures. These students are subjected to punitive measures rather than assistive measures.

Students from diverse backgrounds may find the school experience unpleasant because the adults do not understand their culture and this can result in disengagement and academic failure. These students may not be students with disabilities but instead victims of a school system that does not understand their needs. A lack of understanding of cultural differences and misperceptions of behavior by educators can lead to disproportionate representation of students labeled with emotional/behavior disorder (E/BD).

It has been shown that students with emotional/behavioral disorders engage in high levels of reactive emotions such as anger and reactive aggression. Some students may engage in high rates of reactive aggression as a way to combat prolonged victimization that they have suffered and exhibit this aggression through bullying. They bully because they have been victims of bullying themselves.

This can explain why some students with emotional/behavioral disorders exhibit high levels of bullying and have been over-represented in the bullying dynamic. These children are both victims and engage in bullying themselves. Higher rates of bullying for students with emotional/behavioral disorders can be a manifestation of their disability and may be classified as reactive aggression (Rose and Espelage, 2012).

COMORBIDITY

The most common types of emotional/behavioral disorders are broken down into two key categories, internalizing and externalizing. Internalizing behaviors include depression, anxiety, social withdrawal, and somatic problems. The fact that these are internalizing makes the identification of these children difficult because we cannot see the behaviors. Externalizing behaviors include physical and verbal aggression, classroom disruptions, and off-task behaviors. These behaviors are easy to observe and can be operationally defined (Adamson and Wachsmuth, 2014).

Adults view the externalizing behaviors because they can see them and fail to understand that externalizing behaviors can be masking internalizing problems. As children come into today's schools, their needs are very complex and that complexity requires us to provide them a thorough evaluation. Educators need to be careful not to assume that the externalizing behaviors are the child's only problems. We often oversimplify behavior and the reasons for it and we underestimate the severity of the needs of the children coming in to our schools.

With the major school shooting that occurred in Parkland, Florida, in 2018, an investigation of the background of the young man who was the perpetrator showed that he had been diagnosed with depression, ADHD, possible autism, and emotional/behavioral disability. As a result, policymakers are calling for better mental health services (Wallman, McMahon, O'Matz, and Bryan, 2018).

Learning disabilities are common among students with emotional/behavioral disorders (Mattson, Hooper, and Carlson 2006). A learning disability, not treated, can contribute to the diagnosis of an emotional/behavioral disorder. When the student has a learning disability, the student can become frustrated and therefore exhibit emotional/behavioral disorders that may be internalizing, externalizing, or both.

The neuropsychological deficits which are characteristic of students with learning disabilities have been found to be common in students diagnosed with emotional/behavioral disorders. Children with externalizing behavior problems showed deficits in language and or attention/executive functions. Those deficits cause problems in both learning and behavior. An early combination of problems with attention/hyperactivity, conduct, and cognitive abilities can result in poor scholastic outcomes (Mattson, Hooper, and Carlson, 2006).

Language difficulties have been found common among children with various mental health problems. A number of studies have substantiated this (Spira, Bracken, and Fische, 2005; Cohen, 2001). Lundervold, Heimann, and Manger (2008) found that primary school teachers showed a high degree of awareness of the language functioning of their students and the accompanying behavioral and emotional problems that students with language problems exhibited.

As Kauffman and Landrum (2009) state, "Regardless of whether psychiatric or dimensional classification systems are used, researchers and clinicians frequently find that children and youth exhibit more than one type of problem or disorder" (p. 119). They point out that multiple classifications may be more common than single classifications. Important to note is that comorbidity of behavioral and learning problems makes effective treatment of one in the absence of treatment of the other extremely difficult and can be impossible.

PSYCHIATRIC CONDITIONS

Psychiatric conditions exist along a continuum with some more severe than others. The presenting behaviors can vary from minor to very serious problems (Kauffman and Landrum, 2009). It is estimated that one in five students may have mental illness (Merz, 2017–2018). On the extreme end of psychiatric conditions are those children who exhibit psychotic behaviors in the form of schizophrenia. The child's perception of reality is significantly different than actual reality. It is essentially a disorder of thinking and perception. Children with schizophrenia can exhibit delusions, bizarre behavior, sometimes including hallucinations. These are rare in preadolescents and some children actually believe they are being controlled by alien forces (Kauffman and Hallahan, 2009).

Psychiatric conditions are labeled through the use of the DSM-5. We continue to look for the most appropriate ways to diagnose these conditions. Some people believe that children will be stigmatized by the labels, yet the labels help us to provide appropriate care and educational services.

There is some evidence that maternal depression during pregnancy can result in emotional and behavioral disorders among offspring (Leis et al., 2014). Research has previously focused on postpartum depression while less has been done in the area of depression and anxiety during pregnancy. These symptoms impact children's development and mental health. Researchers have found a modest association between prenatal mental health and later emotional and behavioral difficulties in children (Leis, Heron, Stuart, and Mendelson, 2014).

Anxiety disorders are a neurobiological condition that impact 10 to 20 percent of children in the general population and 6 to 10 percent of children in schools meet the criteria for an anxiety disorder (Killu and Crundwell, 2016). The disorder can manifest itself as seen in phobias, separation fears, and obsessive compulsive behaviors. Anxiety disorder is often non-diagnosed, but the teacher will see the behaviors in the classroom. It is reported to be the most common psychiatric disorder in children (McKibben, 2017).

Obsessive compulsive disorder (OCD) is the fourth most common psychiatric disorder among youth (Sloman, Gallant, and Storch, 2007). Heyman and colleagues (2001) reported that OCD may affect two to three of every 1,000 children ages five to fifteen. Many times these children are diagnosed with emotional disturbance, but some believe it is very important to differentiate it from a behavioral or conduct disorder because it is a neurobiological condition. These children struggle with social interactions because they may feel isolated and may alienate themselves from their peers (Leininger et al., 2010).

We have an increasing population of children who are victims of neglect, abuse, and maltreatment. Seventy-five percent of children who are victims of maltreatment are under the age of twelve (Whitted, Delavega, and Lennon-Dearing, 2013). It is estimated that 81 percent of children who enter foster care have serious problems with mental health compared to 8 to 22 percent of children diagnosed with mental health problems in the general population (Simms et al., 2000). Children who are abused or neglected are more vulnerable to post-traumatic stress disorder, attention deficit hyperactivity disorder, and conduct disorder (Anda et al., 2007).

In 2012, the Centers for Disease Control reported that when children are maltreated during infancy or early childhood, it can interfere with brain development, which can then cause physical, mental, and emotional problems such as sleep disturbances, panic disorder, and attention deficit disorder. Children who are maltreated have difficulty regulating their emotions and understanding the emotions of others (Whitted et al., 2013).

COMMON PERCEPTIONS ABOUT THE STUDENTS

Unfortunately, because the disability of an individual with emotional/behavioral disorders is not visible to the human eye, many people do not understand it. Society finds it difficult to understand what we can't see, and depression, anxiety, and obsessive compulsive disorder are not apparent to the eye and therefore people don't see that there is anything wrong with the individual. The individual then acts out and they can't understand why because they look "normal," but they are not. This contributes to the stigma of having a mental illness.

There is still a stigma to mental illness. For years, individuals with mental illness were either hidden at home or were institutionalized and not accepted by society. Many insurance policies did not cover, and some still do not cover, mental health problems.

To avoid stigmatizing these students and their families, we must be very cautious that we don't make inappropriate assumptions about students.

> False assumption: These children are just acting "bad" and they really could control their own behavior.
>
> Fact: These children oftentimes cannot control their own actions as much as they would like to, and we need to have a better understanding on what may be precipitating the behavior. Later in this book you will be learning about the importance of conducting a functional assessment to determine what is driving the behavior. We cannot help our students without having a thorough understanding about their needs.
>
> False assumption: It is all their parents' fault.

Fact: Many of the parents, of children with emotional/behavioral disorders, are trying as hard as they can and need strong supports, not criticism from us. I remember working with many parents who tried everything that was ever recommended and regardless of what they did, the children still had problems. It is easy for us to criticize the parent, but we must remember that we are not living with the many challenges that these parents face.

We work with children during a school day when we are alert and ready to work with them. The parent has the child the majority of the day and evening when they may very well be tired after working all day and then come home and face a child who has significant needs. While the parents may also have mental health problems themselves, we cannot jump to conclusions and blame them for the problems that the child has.

False assumption: If they are just disciplined better, they will outgrow their problems.

Fact: These children will not outgrow problems without significant positive and multifaceted interventions. They don't outgrow their disabilities and may struggle throughout their lifetimes.

TEN TEACHING TIPS

As teachers strive to understand the challenges these children face and why they may behave the way they do, teachers should do the following:

1. Thoroughly review the records of the student to gather as much information as possible.
2. Talk with previous teachers to find out what strategies were most successful in supporting the student.
3. Work positively with the parents to learn as much as you can about your students.
4. Observe the child closely to determine what the child responds positively to and what triggers upset the student.
5. Interview the student to determine the child's insights into what helps them and what hinders them.
6. Read as much as you can about the conditions that the student may have.

7. Watch the student closely for any changes in behavior.

8. Elicit the support and assistance of the school psychologist, school social worker, school counselor, and others that may provide insight into the challenges the student faces.

9. Find out whether the student is involved with other agencies and seek permission to speak with those agencies about the needs of the student.

10. Monitor your own behavior to determine whether you are practicing understanding and respect for the student.

QUESTIONS FOR DISCUSSION

1. Think about whether there has been anyone in your family with an emotional/behavioral disorder. How did you know they had problems and what interventions were utilized?

2. What negative statements have you heard about students with emotional/behavioral disorders? What is your response to those statements?

3. How will you research the mental health concerns that your students have in order for you to better assist them?

REFERENCES

Adamson, R. and Wachsmuth, S. (2014). A review of direct observation research within the past decade in the field of emotional and behavior disorders. *Behavioral Disorders, 39(4),* 181–89.

Anda, R., Brown, D., Felitti, V., Bremner, J., Dube, S., and Giles, W. (2007). Adverse childhood experiences and prescribed psychotropic medications in adults. *American Journal of Preventative Medicine, 32(5),* 389–94.

Centers for Disease Control and Prevention (CDC) (2012). *Child maltreatment: Consequences.* Retrieved November 6, 2012 from www.childwelfare.gov/pubs/factsheets/long_term_consequences.cfm.

Cohen, N. (2001). *Language and psychopathology in infants, children and adolescents.* Thousand Oaks, CA: Sage.

Heyman, I., Fontbonne, E., Simmons, H., Ford, T., Meltzer, H., and Goodman, R. (2001). Prevalence of obsessive-compulsive disorder in the British nationwide survey of child mental health. *The British Journal of Psychiatry, 179,* 324–29.

Killu, K. and Crundwell, R. (2016). Students with anxiety in the classroom: Educational accommodations and interventions. *Beyond Behavior, 25(2),* 28–40.

Kauffman, J., and Landrum, T. (2009). *Characteristics of emotional and behavioral disorders of children and youth.* Upper Saddle River, NJ: Pearson.

Leininger, M., Dyches, T., Prater, M., Heath, M., and Bascom, S. (2010). Books portraying characters with obsessive-compulsive disorder. *Teaching Exceptional Children, 42(4),* 22–28.

Leis, J., Heron, J., Stuart, E., and Mendelson, T. (2014). Associations between maternal mental health and child emotional and behavioral problems: Does prenatal mental health matter? *Journal of Abnormal Child Psychology, 42,* 161–71.

Lundervold, A., Heimann, M., and Manger, T. (2008). Behavior-emotional characteristics of primary school children rated as having language problems. *British Journal of Educational Psychology, 78(5),* 67–80.

Mattison, R., Hooper, S., and Carlson, G. (2006). Neuropsychological characteristics of special education students with serious emotional/behavioral disorders. *Behavioral Disorders, 31(2),* 176–88.

McKibben, S. (2017). Helping ease student anxiety. *ASCD Education Update, 59(8),* 1, 4–5.

Merz, S. (2017–2018). Who in your class needs help? *Educational Leadership, 75(4),* 12–17.

Moreno, G., Wong-Lo, M., Short, M., and Bullock, L. (2014). Implementing a culturally attuned functional behavioral assessment to understand and address challenging behaviors demonstrated by students from diverse backgrounds. *Emotional and Behavioral Difficulties, 19(4),* 343–55.

Rose, C. and Espelage, D. (2012). Risk and protective factors associated with the bullying involvement of students with emotional and behavioral disorders. *Behavioral Disorders, 37(3),* 133–48.

Simms, M., Dubowitz, H., and Szilgyi, M. (2000). Health care needs of children in the foster care system. *Pediatrics 106(4),* 909–18.

Sloman, G., Gallant, J., and Storch, E. (2007). A school-based treatment model for pediatric obsessive compulsive disorder. *Child Psychiatry and Human Development, 38,* 303–19.

Spira, E., Bracken, S., and Fische, J. (2005). Predicting improvement after first-grade reading difficulties: The effects of oral language, emergent literacy, and behavior skills. *Developmental Psychology, 41,* 225–34.

Wallman, B., McMahon, P., O'Matz, M., and Bryan, S. (2018). "He would stare into your soul." *South Florida Sun Sentinel,* Sunday, February 25, 2018.

Whitted, K., Delavega, E., and Lennon-Dearing, R. (2013). The youngest victims of violence: Examining the mental health needs of young children who are involved in the child welfare and juvenile justice systems. *Child Adolescent Social Work Journal, 30,* 181–95.

2

PREVENTION, SCREENING, EVALUATION, AND PLACEMENT

Tyler was assessed and subsequently diagnosed in first grade with an attention deficit hyperactivity disorder (ADHD) by a local child psychiatrist. Tyler is usually off-task, defiant, noncompliant, and is frequently disruptive in class. His third-grade teacher, Ms. Green, with the assistance of the school's behavior specialist, has tried many interventions and approaches to encourage Tyler to improve his behavior. His off-task, defiant, disruptive, and noncompliant behavior prevents him from achieving up to his potential, prohibits other students from doing their work, and requires a disproportionate amount of time from Ms. Green, her assistant, and other members of the school staff. Ms. Green has held three conferences with Tyler's mother during the last six months regarding her son's behavior. During each of these conferences, the mother has said that Tyler's disruptive behavior is caused by her recent separation from her husband. She contends that Tyler was close to his father, and he has been getting increasingly more disruptive and defiant since his father moved out. Ms. Green feels that Tyler should have an evaluation for E/BD. Ms. Green has discussed Tyler's behavior with the school's special education team. They feel it is time to schedule a conference with Tyler's mother to receive consent for an E/BD evaluation. During the conference it is obvious that Tyler's mother is frustrated and is out of answers. Consequently, Tyler's mom signs consent for an E/BD evaluation.

STANDARDS

CEC Initial Teacher Preparation Standard 1.0—Beginning special education professionals understand how exceptionalities may interact with development and learning and use this knowledge to provide meaningful and challenging learning experiences for individuals with exceptionalities.

CEC Initial Teacher Preparation Standard 4.0—Beginning special education professionals use multiple methods of assessment and data sources in making educational decisions.

CEC Initial Teacher Preparation Standard 7.0—Beginning special education professionals collaborate with families, other educators, related services providers, individuals with exceptionalities, and personnel from community agencies in culturally responsive ways to address the needs of individuals with exceptionalities across a range of learning experiences.

CHAPTER OBJECTIVES

Readers will be able:

1. To explain the purpose of screening and of evaluation.
2. To explain the purpose of PBIS and the three tiers of it.
3. To list the steps in conducting an FBA.
4. To list the steps in developing a behavior intervention plan (BIP).
5. To explain how the full continuum of placement options must be considered when determining placement for a student with E/BD.

KEY VOCABULARY TERMS

Prevention—To assist students who are having difficulty before the potential behavior problems turn into a disability.

Primary Prevention—Procedures designed to keep a disorder from occurring.

Secondary Prevention—Procedures implemented soon after a problem has been detected. Designed to reverse or correct a problem or prevent it from getting worse.

Tertiary Prevention—Procedures designed to keep a severe or chronic disorder from causing complications or overwhelming the individuals or others.

FBA—A process of data collection to describe antecedents, behaviors, consequences (ABCs) to determine the function or communicative intent of the behavior.

ABC Analysis—The major purpose of the A-B-C (antecedent-behavior-consequence) analysis is to get a reliable record of the antecedents and consequences that are typically associated with a problem behavior under normal circumstances. This information is then structured by listing each problem behavior and the events that occur immediately before it (i.e., antecedents) and immediately after (consequences) to identify any patterns that might indicate a functional relationship.

Interview—Interviews, asking parents, students, and teachers specific questions regarding students' behaviors at school or home, provides information that can be used to assist in the evaluation process.

Behavior Intervention Plan—A behavior intervention plan is a plan based on an FBA. The FBA's major purpose is to determine the function of the child's challenging behavior. Once the function is determined, an effective behavior management program can be developed to serve the same function of the target behavior.

Screening—Screening is a brief procedure that samples a few behaviors across skills or domains with the general purpose of identifying students whose behaviors may be indicative of a serious problem and who should be assessed more thoroughly.

IEP—An IEP is a written document that records the essential components of an eligible student's educational program.

Placement—To ensure students are placed in the least restrictive environment (LRE), school districts must ensure that continuums of alternative placements are available.

FUNCTIONAL BEHAVIOR ASSESSMENT (FBA)

The functional behavioral assessment (FBA), mandated by law (IDEA 1997; IDEA 2004) for use in schools, is a strategy for the development of intervention plans for students with disabilities. IDEA 1997 required that when a student with a disability exhibits challenging behavior that interferes with their behavior or the behaviors of others, then the individualized education (IEP) team must conduct an FBA and develop a BIP.

While IDEA 2004 or its regulations detailed what challenging behavior are covered under the statute, Drasgow and Yell (2001) determined through previous litigation that these behaviors include: (a) disruptive behaviors that impair the teacher from teaching and other students from learning, (b) noncompliance, (c) abuse of property, and (d) verbal abuse and/or aggression towards students and staff.

Students who engage in these behaviors are candidates for FBAs and BIPs. FBAs should be completed as part of the evaluation process of IEP development, and the BIP should be implemented into the IEP for all students with E/BD.

An accurate interpretation of the FBA requirement of IDEA requires that an FBA be conducted when students with disabilities are subject to disciplinary action. However, FBAs should be conducted as a proactive measure to support students with challenging behavior when their behavior impacts their learning and the learning of others and not just wait until disciplinary actions are necessary. Appendix A depicts when an FBA should be conducted.

While the FBA can take on different forms, the underlying intention is to determine the function or purpose that a challenging behavior serves for an individual student. The process of FBA includes gathering information about antecedents and consequences that are linked to the occurrence of challenging behavior (Miltenberger, 2012). This information improves the effectiveness and proficiency of the BIP. An FBA should identify the following types of information (Kern, O'Neill, and Starosta, 2005; O'Neill, Albin, Storey, Horner, and Sprague, 2015):

1. The assessment begins with the development of an operational definition which must be observable and measurable. The following steps will help determine the adequacy of operational definitions:

2. Can you count times of the behavior, or measure how long it takes before the behavior occurs again?

3. Did you use observable and measurable terms in defining the behavior?

4. Will a stranger know exactly what behavior to look for after reading your definition?

5. Can you explain what the behavior is not? (i.e., give non-examples of the behavior).

6. Can you break the behavior into smaller specific and more observable units?

7. Most behaviors happen because there is a consequence maintaining them. Challenging behaviors are no different. Challenging behaviors (e.g., disruption) basically occurs because there is some consequence maintaining it (e.g., attention from peers in the form of laughing). Consequently, every FBA must include information regarding the consequences that are maintaining the challenging behaviors.

FUNCTIONS OF BEHAVIOR

The functions, or consequences, of challenging behavior may include:

- Attention—to get focused attention from parents, teachers, siblings, peers, or other people that are around them.
- Escape/Avoidance—to get out of doing something he/she does not want to do.
- Sensory/Self Stimulation—behaviors because it feels good to them.
- Seeking Access to Tangible Materials—to get a preferred item or participate in an enjoyable activity.
- Power—to gain control, vengeance, or demonstrate intimidation.

The individual's behavior may be controlled by multiple functions or be unable to be specified (Beavers and Iwata, 2011; Mueller, Nkosi, and Hine, 2011).

FBA data includes antecedents and antecedent conditions that are associated with the challenging behavior. Setting events data is also part of the FBA process. Setting events are different from antecedents in that they do not trigger behavior themselves, but instead they alter the probability that the antecedent will evoke the behavior. An FBA should identify setting events because of their relationship to predicting and preventing challenging behavior.

The rationale for conducting an FBA is to identify the factors that predict and maintain the challenging behavior so that the function (e.g., shouting, aggression, or avoiding work) of the challenging behavior can be determined (Carr et al., 1994; O'Neill et al., 2015). An FBA is the first and most significant step toward developing a BIP because it directs the selection of intervention strategies that are associated (a) with the purpose of the behavior and (b) with the daily routines of each specific student (Yell et al., 2013).

Conducting the Functional Behavioral Assessment

An FBA should accomplish five outcomes (O'Neill et al., 2015):

a. Operational definition(s) of the challenging behaviors,
b. Descriptions of the setting events and antecedents (e.g., times, locations, activities) that predict the occurrence and nonoccurrence of the challenging behavior,
c. Descriptions of the consequences for the challenging behavior,
d. Verification of the consequences through direct observations, and
e. Summary hypothesis statements that serve as the basis for designing the positive behavior support plan.

There are three standard methods for conducting the FBA and accomplishing these five outcomes: indirect methods, direct observation methods, and experimental methods (Miltenberger, 2012). These three methods are associated and usually are conducted in the order in which they are listed below.

Indirect Methods

Indirect methods consist of gathering information on the students' challenging behavior from individuals who have direct contact with the students and know the student well. These data can take the form of referral information and school records, completing behavior rating scales and checklists, and conducting interviews. The purpose of indirect measures is to collect a large amount of data in a short period of time by reviewing various sources of existing information. The gathering of information obtained from indirect measures is the beginning point of an FBA and direction and focus with proceeding with other measures (Yell et al., 2013).

Referral Information and School Records

Gathering information from a student's teacher or teachers who have referred the student for special education services or consultation is the first step of an FBA. Teachers can obtain additional relevant information about the challenging behavior by conducting a systematic review of school records (Gresham et al., 2001). This information should include the student's name, age, gender, current placement(s), and reason for referral. The reason for referral should describe the challenging behavior in detail and what strategies have been used to remediate the challenging behavior (Chandler and Dahlquist, 2014).

Behavior Rating Scales and Checklists

We suggest two useful checklists that teachers may want to consider using: The Motivational Assessment Scale (MAS) and the Problem Behavior Questionnaire (PBQ). The MAS is a sixteen-item scale that evaluates setting events and maintaining consequences (i.e., positive or negative reinforcement). The questionnaire is designed to assess the function(s) of challenging behavior to assist in the FBA process (Durrand and Crimmins, 1988). The scoring is similar to the MAS. Raters are asked to rate the frequency observed for each item (e.g., never, always).

The PBQ has fifteen items (Lewis, Scott, and Sugai, 1994). The scoring and administration are similar to the MAS. Behavior rating scales and checklists may provide some preliminary information regarding setting events, antecedents, and consequences related to the occurrence of problem behavior (Yell et al., 2013).

Interviews

Teachers can utilize interviews to get a primary understanding of the challenging behaviors and their setting events, antecedents, predictors, and consequences. The teachers can fall back with their experience with the child. The teachers can interview other teachers, professionals who are most familiar with the child's challenging behavior, or family members.

The teachers can interview the child if they feel confident that they can get reliable and valid information from the child. In general, the interviewer asks individuals to describe three things: (a) the physical description of the challenging behavior, (b) the circumstances that predict the occurrence or nonoccurrence of challenging behavior, and (c) the reaction that the challenging behavior evokes from others (Carr et al., 1994; Lewis et al., 1994; O'Neill et al., 2015).

The objective of the interviewer is to get people to answer questions about environmental situations and events without interferences or interruptions (Miltenberger, 2012). For example, the interviewer may ask the teacher what happens immediately after she gives Molly, a student with challenging behavior, a task demand (e.g., to clean up after themselves after free time when it is time to start math). The teacher responds, "Molly gets upset when I ask her to do something she does not want to do."

The rationale of these questions is to secure enough information so that patterns start to emerge. Teachers then analyze these patterns of behavior to develop hypotheses about the function of the challenging behavior.

The central objective and goals of the FAI is to develop an operational definition, to allow a quick review of a large number of potential setting events, antecedents, consequences, and to provide a starting point to initiate observational FBA methods. Based on this information, the interviewer can start developing a tentative hypothesis, or summary statement, about the consequences that maintain the challenging behavior (Yell et al., 2013).

Summary Hypothesis Statements

The objective of the indirect FBA methods is to obtain information about the setting events, antecedents, and consequences associated with the challenging behavior. FBA indirect methods do not substantiate the function of challenging behavior; consequently, they lead to summary hypothesis statements regarding the potential function of the challenging behavior.

The summary statement is a testable hypothesis that provides a connection between the FBA and the BIP process it (a) suggests which setting events, antecedents, and consequences should be manipulated in order to decrease the challenging behavior and (b) reveals which new behavior should be taught to replace the challenging behavior (Crone and Horner, 2003). The objective of preceding FBA methods is to substantiate the accuracy of the indirect FBA information. See Appendix B for examples of summary questions to ask.

Direct Observation Methods

There are two direct observation strategies commonly used: scatter plot evaluation and collecting A-B-C observations.

Scatter Plot Evaluation

Challenging behavior typically is not evenly distributed across the day. Instead, it tends to occur more often at times than other times. A scatter plot assessment (SPA) can be used to determine when challenging behavior is most likely and unlikely to occur (Touchette, MacDonald, and Langer, 1985), especially when the challenging behavior occurs frequently and seemingly random.

A scatter plot is a grid that is distributed into time intervals with corresponding spaces to code behaviors across days. Each time interval on the grid can be filled in to represent whether challenging behavior occurred at a high, low, or zero rate.

A teacher can analyze a completed grid to determine if the challenging behavior is related with time of day, absence, or presence of specific individuals, activities or events, physical or social settings, or any combination of these factors (Yell et al., 2013).

A-B-C Analysis

The primary purpose of the A-B-C observation is to receive a reliable record of the antecedents and consequences that are typically related with the challenging behavior under normal conditions (Bijou et al., 1968). A-B-C observations are more reliable information than indirect methods because they rely less on memory or subjective conclusions.

A-B-C observations consist of an individual directly observing the challenging behavior in the natural setting where the challenging behavior takes place. The observer records the immediate antecedents and consequences each time the challenging behavior occurs.

This data is then structured by listing each challenging behavior and the events that occur immediately before (i.e., antecedents) and immediately after it (i.e., consequences) to identify any patterns that might indicate a functional relationship (Alberto and Troutman, 2013). O'Neill et al. (2015) have developed a thorough A-B-C analysis form (FAO) that can be used to record observational data.

Guidelines for Interpreting Data from the FAO

- Examine the data to decide which behaviors are occurring, how often they are occurring, and whether some or all of the behaviors seem to be co-occurring regularly;
- Examine the data to see whether behaviors are consistently occurring during particular time periods, and whether particular predictors are consistently related to the occurrence of particular behaviors during specific time periods;
- Consider the perceived functions and actual consequences to identify the probable functions of different behaviors and the consequences that may be maintaining them; and
- Based on the observation data, decide whether your initial summary statements seem valid, whether they should be revised or discarded and whether you need to develop additional statements (O'Neill et al., 2015).

The A-B-C analysis should take place in multiple settings or under different conditions (e.g., during math, language, or physical education instruction) so as to gather information about the situations where the challenging behaviors are likely to occur (Desrochers and Fallon, 2014). Based on the analysis of this information, a function of the students' challenging behavior can be determined.

Experimental Method

A functional analysis is an experimental method that tests hypothesis about behavioral function by systematically manipulating specific antecedent conditions and then by providing consequences for challenging behavior to determine whether or not they impact the challenging behavior (Baer, Wolf, and Risley, 1968; Skinner, 1953).

Functional analysis directly tests an association among environmental events, consequences, and challenging behavior. Functional analysis can be time consuming and energy-consuming but in some cases, it may be the only way to determine an accurate assessment of challenging behaviors (Yell et al., 2013).

A functional analysis should always be conducted by an individual trained in the procedure due to the fact that it involves creating circumstances that may provoke the challenging behavior (O'Neill et al., 2015). Educators should note that functional analysis should follow very precise procedures to be accurate and that it may evoke challenging behaviors (e.g., throwing computers).

BEHAVIOR INTERVENTION PLANS (BIP)

Characteristics of Behavior Intervention Plans

BIP should be based on FBA (i.e., instead of disrupting the class, ask for assistance when you get frustrated) and

1. Include a replacement behavior(s) based on the function of the target behavior.
2. Address two parallel intervention strategies; one to teach and support the replacement behavior and one to correct or reduce the target behavior.
3. Sometimes students lack the skill or choose not to comply because they have been reinforced to maintain the behavior.
4. Behavior intervention plans should operationally describe the target and replacement behaviors.
5. Include intervention goals and strategies that prevent, replace, and manage target behaviors.

6. Include mechanisms for ensuring implementation and progress.

Besides following these general rules, the behavior plan must include means to modify antecedent conditions, setting events, and academic needs that may bring about the challenging behavior. Changes in teaching strategies may be necessary to make these modifications.

Using the Competing Behavior Model to Build Positive Behavior Intervention Plans

The competing behavior model (O'Neill et al., 2015) is a three-step approach for creating BIPs that are directly related to FBA data. First, the FBA information is condensed into a precise summary hypothesis statement. This statement is organized based on a behavioral sequence of setting events, antecedents, behavior, and consequence that are central to applied behavior analysis (ABA). The summary statement serves as the backbone of the BIP, and all interventions are logically associated to it (Yell et al., 2013).

The second step of the competing behavior model is to select alternative or competing behaviors and the consequence related with each. There are two forms of alternative behaviors in this model. Replacement behaviors result in the same outcome or consequence, as the problem behavior. For example, if a student rips up their math worksheet and throws it on the floor to escape task demands, then the replacement behavior for that student may be to ask for help that reduces the punitive nature of the task. Replacement behaviors empower students to impact their environment in a prosocial manner so that they no longer have to resort to the challenging behavior.

The other type of alternative behavior is the desirable behavior that should occur, which has a different function of the challenging behavior. In the earlier example, the desired behavior would be that the student completes the academic task. Finishing the task is not the same as escaping the task.

The third step of the competing behavior model is to identify changes that will make the challenging behavior irrelevant, inefficient, and ineffective. We make the problem behavior irrelevant by altering the conditions that evoke it. Consequently, if a student engages in challenging behavior to escape academic demands, altering the features of the academic demands so they are no longer aversive makes escape irrelevant.

Setting Event Strategies

The purpose of setting event strategies is to prevent the challenging behavior from occurring by alternating the events that have made it more likely that the challenging behavior will occur in the first place. Recall that setting events are different from antecedents because they do not initiate challenging behavior themselves but instead alter the probability that the antecedents will evoke the challenging behavior.

For instance, if a student was more likely to demonstrate challenging behavior when they came to school hungry, an appropriate setting event strategy would be to give the student breakfast at school, thus removing the event that put them in a bad mood and made it likely that an antecedent would trigger challenging behaviors.

Similarly, if a student came to school tired because they had little sleep the prior night, an appropriate setting event strategy would be to allow the student to put their head down on their desk before school starts (Yell et al., 2013).

Antecedent Strategies

Antecedent strategies prevent the challenging behavior from occurring by modifying or addressing the circumstances or events that trigger or set off the problem behavior. Usually, these strategies will organize the environment so that the possibility that the student will encounter the antecedent will be minimized.

Examples of some environmental changes include (a) alternating the physical setting, (b) enriching the environment, (c) modifying the curriculum, and (d) increasing the student's choices for an activity (O'Neill et al., 2015). Challenging behavior will be neutralized because the situations that set the occasion for problem behavior to arise are altered in ways that eliminate the need for these behaviors to occur.

Teaching Strategies

The purpose of teaching strategies is to enable students to learn new skills to impact their environment in alternative ways that are socially acceptable. Teaching strategies may consist of direct instruction, prompting, cueing, or shaping. A teacher may utilize a combination of instructional strategies to foster acquisition of a new behavior (Yell et al., 2013).

Consequence Strategies

Consequence strategies refer to providing reinforcement to increase all prosocial behaviors and withholding reinforcement that maintains the challenging behavior. Remember that challenging behavior continues because it is being reinforced, and the purpose of the FBA is to identify reinforcers that are maintaining the occurrence of the challenging behavior.

The purpose of the BIP is to increase prosocial behaviors identified in the BIP. Therefore, it is the teacher's obligation to reinforce these newly acquired behaviors. If the BIP is appropriately developed, then it will include several strategies that make the challenging behavior irrelevant and less likely to occur (Yell et al., 2013).

Fidelity of the BIP

One of the most problematic challenges for effective behavioral support is getting all of the components of the BIP implemented with precision. The individuals who developed the BIP may not be the people who implement it. The following actions can jeopardize the integrity of a BIP: inadequate faculty and staff training; lack of administrative support; vague definitions of the challenging behaviors; incorrect interpretation of the data; insufficient intervention to deal with the behavior; incorrect application of the intervention plan; failure to monitor the implementation of the plan, to evaluate the impact of the plan, and then adjust it for different settings; and inadequate system-wide support and technical assistance (Jones, Dohrn, and Dunn, 2004).

Monitoring the BIP

It is critical that teachers and staff collect quantitative data to document a student's progress and to make data-based decisions with this data. It is important to collect data on both target (i.e., talk outs) and replacement behaviors (i.e., raising hand to contribute during class).

Screening and Assessment

Screening

Screening is a brief procedure that samples a few behaviors across skills or domains (Overton, 2009), with the general objective of identifying students whose behavior may be indicative of a serious problem and who should have been assessed more thoroughly. Concisely, screening should be utilized to determine the need for additional assessment. Screening is often validated by the argument that early identification will lead to prevention.

The instrument known as the Systematic Screening for Behavior Disorders (SSBD) (Walker and Severson, 1990) is considered a screening device. It is designed for use in elementary school based on the conclusion that teacher judgment is a valid and effective method for identifying students with E/BD (Walker et al., 1994).

Walker and Severson (1990) described the multiple-gating assessment as a procedure that consists of a series of progressively more precise assessment that organizes a multimethod assessment to aid in reliable decision-making. "Multiple gating gradually narrows the larger pool until those individuals who are highly likely to exhibit the (learning and behavior problems) in question are identified" (Merrell, 1994, p. 37).

In the first step or gate of the SSBD, the teacher lists and rank-orders students with externalizing and internalizing behavior problems, listing those who best fit the descriptions, and rank-ordering them from most to least like the descriptions of externalizing and internalizing behaviors (Kauffman and Landrum, 2013).

The second step necessitates that the teacher complete two checklists for the three highest ranked students on each list; those who have passed through the first "gate." One checklist asks the teacher to articulate whether the pupil exhibited specific behaviors during the past month (e.g., "steals, "has tantrums," "uses obscene language or swears").

These behaviors compose a Critical Events Index (CEI) of behaviors that, even if they occur at a low frequency constitute "behavioral earthquakes" that place children at a very high risk of being identified as having E/BD (Gresham, MacMillan, and Bocian, 1996).

The other checklists require that the teacher assess how often ("never," "sometimes," "frequently") each student demonstrates certain characteristics (e.g., follows classroom rules, cooperates with peers in group activities or situations).

The third step requires observations of students whose scores on the checklist surpass established norms; those who have passed through the second "gate." Students are observed in the classroom and on the playground by a school professional other than the typical classroom teacher (e.g., a school psychologist, counselor, or resource teacher).

Classroom observations indicate the extent to which the student meets academic expectations; playground observations assess the quality and nature of social behavior. These direct observations, in addition to teacher ratings, are then used to decide whether the student has problems that warrant full evaluation for special education (an evaluation for E/BD) (Kauffman and Landrum, 2013).

The procedures that Walker (1994) and his colleagues developed are the most fully comprehensive screening system currently developed for use in school settings. Lane (2010) referred to the SSBD as the "gold standard" among systematic screeners for E/BD. The CEI (Critical Events Index) alone has been utilized to reliably distinguish typical children from those at risk and those who have been identified as having been identified as having E/BD (Kauffman and Landrum, 2013).

DEFINITION OF E/BD

Prior to the 1997 reauthorization of the Individuals with Disabilities Act (IDEA), the term for the special education category for children with E/BD was serious emotional disturbance (SED). In the IDEA Amendments of 1997, the word "serious" was dropped from the definition. Consequently, the federal definition was changed to Emotional Disturbance (ED).

There were no changes to the terminology in IDEA 2004. Federal law defines emotional disturbance as a condition in which one or more of the following characteristics are exhibited over a long period of time (over six months) and to a marked degree and that adversely affects educational performance:

a. An inability to learn that cannot be explained by intellectual, sensory, and health factors.

    b. An inability to build or maintain satisfactory interpersonal relationships with peers and teachers.

    c. Inappropriate types of behaviors and feelings under normal circumstances.

    d. A general pervasive mood or unhappiness or depression.

    e. A tendency to develop physical symptoms or fears associated with personal or school problems (IDEA regulations, 34 C. F. R. § 300.8(c)(4)).

The IDEA definition also includes schizophrenia, but does not apply to children who are socially maladjusted unless it is determined that they have an emotional disturbance.

The five characteristics of emotional disturbance do not necessarily appear in all children and youth labeled as E/BD, however, the behavior needs to be severe, chronic, and frequent. The five criteria are listed below with descriptive behaviors that are associated with each.

1. An inability to learn that cannot be explained by intellectual, sensory, or health factors.
2. An inability to build or maintain satisfactory interpersonal relationships with peers and teachers.
3. Inappropriate types of behaviors and feelings under normal circumstances.
4. A general pervasive mood or unhappiness or depression.
5. A tendency to develop physical symptoms or fears associated with personal or school problems (Jones et al., 2004).

An evaluation of a student for E/BD requires a multilevel group of assessments in order to not falsely identify a student for this disability and to not over-identify students from minority groups. The requirements for a full evaluation to determine eligibility include:

- Medical information in the form of medical statements or health assessments, behavior records indicating there are no medical issues that could be the cause of the behavior problems.
- Behavior records including referrals, discipline records, and attendance records, or previous referral for special education.
- Academic performance records including teacher reports, grade work samples, and standardized achievement tests.

- Observations in a variety of settings (e.g., academic setting; including a setting where the behavior takes place; a setting in which behavior is reported to be minimal; an unstructured setting such as lunch or recess.
- Interviews with teachers, parents, students, and other caregivers.
- Functional behavioral assessments and any BIPs.
- Formal behavior rating scales with staff and parents.
- IQ testing.
- Psychological evaluation.
- Documentation of previously utilized interventions (Jones et al., 2004).

ASSESSMENT TECHNIQUES

Records Review

The evaluator should review grades and disciplinary referrals from the previous year(s) to determine if the student has had academic and social problems in previous grades. Changes in grades, teacher comments on student behavior, and inconsistencies or fluctuations across subject areas and grade levels should be reviewed (Christner, Bolton, and Zarabba, 2011).

If significant difficulties are not noted, then the evaluator needs to consider why the student is experiencing difficulties at this time. The following are other ways to inspect the records: (a) history of school changes, (b) pattern of absences, truancies, suspensions, disciplinary actions, time in nurse's office, (c) pattern of grades over the years (e.g., always good, gradual, in decline?), (d) pattern of group test scores, including IQ and achievement results, (e) specific parameters of the problem behaviors as described by others, contact with school social worker or counselor, and (f) previous special education referrals.

Developmental and Health History

The current developmental functioning of the student is another important area of review (NASP, 2005). Assessing developmental functioning also requires examination of the health history of the student. The district or school nurse is often responsible for collecting and compiling the student's medical and developmental history.

The evaluator should concentrate on locating information pertaining to any identified developmental delays in adaptive behavior (e.g., motor skills, peer relations, language, and self-help skills). Specific information should be sought on any prenatal, delivery or postnatal difficulties, or problems including Apgar scores (Apgar, 1953). In addition to early developmental milestones, the evaluator should also look for previous or current medications as well as chronic health problems, early hospitalizations, childhood diseases, previous neurological difficulties, or accidents (Christner et al., 2011).

Interview Techniques

Interviews are often obtained to get information about the student on a variety of issues and to gain insight into overall pattern of thinking and behaving. The interviewer needs some level of expertise to keep the interviewer session focused throughout.

There are several variations on the interview method; most distinctions are made along a continuum of structured and unstructured or formal or informal. Regardless of the format, interviews, through a series of predetermined questions, should probe for information in one or more of the following areas of functioning and development: social emotional functioning, peer interactions, adult interactions, prosocial skills, and educational functioning.

Teacher Interviews

Interviewing the student's teacher is another critical piece of the evaluation process. The interview process should focus on the teacher's current concerns about the student, focusing on (1) the behaviors of the student within the classroom setting, and (2) the expectations for student behavior. It is critical to keep the interview focused and to help the teacher operationally define concerns and relationship with peers (Christner et al., 2011; Mayer and McGookin, 1977).

Parent Interviews

The parent interview is another opportunity for the evaluator to obtain data regarding student behavior, as well as building rapport and acquiring parent support for school-based interventions. Information provided by the parent can be of critical value in determining the student's behaviors in a setting outside of school. This information can be used to determine the pervasiveness of the E/BD.

Student Interview

Interviewing students can obtain valuable information regarding the student's perception of their behavior at school. Hughes and Baker (1990) recommended that the evaluator should use a combination of open-ended ("Tell me about your classroom?") and direct questions that avoid leading the student ("What happens when your teacher gets angry?"). Interviewing younger students must be appropriate to their developmental and cognitive levels.

Classroom Observations

Classroom observations allow the evaluator to look at actual student behaviors in the classroom setting and to observe dynamics that may be playing a key role in the behavioral difficulties (Merrell, 2008). Failure to engage in a meaningful classroom observation as part of an assessment process for a student with a potential E/BD may result in the subsequent assessment report being considered incomplete or invalid (Tibbetts, 2013).

A systematic review of the classroom context within which behavior occurs, is a critical variable in an educational evaluation of E/BD. This analysis assists in ascertaining to what extent the setting may be contributing to the problem behavior and how aspects of the setting could be changed as part of any recommended interventions (Tibbetts, 2013). Keogh and Speece (1996) ascertained that the classroom setting is seldom taken into account as a source of student difficulties.

Multiple observations on different days and times should be made in order to secure a wide sample of student behavior across as many settings as possible, including recess, lunch, and structured and unstructured classroom times. It is generally recommended that each observation should last at least thirty minutes. Sustained observations across settings may be a highly effective means of identifying behavioral functions.

Behavior Rating Scales

Behavior rating scales are often used in the evaluation of E/BD and developing educational programs for students with E/BD (Jones et al., 2004). Many times, several (teachers, parents, and at times students) individuals complete rating scales, and then the ranges are evaluated to assess the level of agreement about a student's behavior.

When aggregated, ratings by several individuals also diminish the possibility for bias. Furthermore, one should be cautious of making judgments based on the ratings of a single observer, be it parent or teacher (Kaufman and Landrum, 2013). As Pierangelo and Giulani (2006) commented, "Getting various viewpoints, a more comprehensive evaluation of the child's daily functioning can be established" (p. 193). The scores obtained on rating scales can be assessed to norms that are helpful in concluding whether behavior necessitates intervention and in describing or classifying the types of problems a child or youth exhibits (Gresham, 2000).

Behavior rating scales have several advantages as tools to gather information about student behavior, which include: cost and time efficiency, direct comparison of the target child with peers, flexibility for screening and diagnostic purposes, and providing quantitative information leading to the development of an IEP (Jones et al., 2004).

The Devereaux Behavior Rating Scale-School Form appears to relate most directly to the IDEA 2004 definition of ED (Power and Eiraldi, 2000), and the authors stressed that its purpose is to assess behaviors of typical children and adolescents with moderate to severe ED (Naglieri, LeBuffe, and Pfeiffer, 1993). However, the scale contains only forty items, and results should be interpreted with caution.

Student behavior often varies from one setting to another, such as home versus school or one classroom to another. Perspectives or judgments of student behavior can also vary from one person to another; for example, informants may significantly differ in their thresholds for determining that a behavior is a problem (Reid and Maag, 1994).

In addition, many rating scales have been developed with and normed on mainly Caucasian students from middle-class backgrounds. These measures may not be appropriate in the diagnostic assessment of students from minority groups, namely those from lower socioeconomic backgrounds (Power and Eiraldi, 2000). For these reasons, agreement between informants in different situations is likely to be moderate at best (McConaughy and Ritter, 2002).

Rating scales are subject to the same misuse and misinterpretations as any other standardized assessment instrument regarding reliability, validity, inappropriate application, and bias (Pierangelo and Giulani, 2006). Another potential misapplication is to ask teachers or others who aren't sufficiently familiar with a student to complete the rating scale (Kauffman and Landrum, 2013).

Furthermore, Worthen, Borg, and White (1993) reported that there is a tendency for current incidents and behavior to be given disproportionate weight when the rater completes the rating scale. Behavior rating scales should be considered as one piece of information in the assessment of students with E/BD.

DEVELOPING AN IEP FOR A STUDENT IDENTIFIED AS E/BD

IDEA 2004 requires IEP teams addressing behavior problems to attend to the following issues:

- Investigate the need for strategies and interventions and a support system to address any behavior that may impede a student's learning.
- Create a functional behavioral assessment in response to behavior that impacts the child's learning and the learning of others, disciplinary actions, and subsequently develop or revise a behavior intervention plan.
- Development and implementing of positive behavioral support to manage student behaviors.

Writing IEP goals for students identified as E/BD. We recommend writing IEP goals from a prescribed educational framework and using only five goal areas for a student identified as E/BD. They are:

- Academic performance (if applicable, if student has academic deficits)
- Adult and peer relationships
- Building and classroom expectations
- Vocational goals
- Reintegration goals

Placement Decisions (LRE)

Placement decisions are often made for political rather than student-centered purposes. These decisions must be made in light of the least restriction environment and should be based on the student's needs. IEP teams must consider all options on the full continuum of placement options.

IN SUMMARY

To determine whether a student may be eligible for services under the category of emotional disturbance, it is critical that a thorough evaluation be conducted. Before a student is referred, every effort should be made to provide primary and secondary level interventions as part of a PBIS system. If there is knowledge of a disability or suspicion of a disability, the multidisciplinary team must conduct an evaluation to learn as much about the student as possible.

A functional assessment is a critical component in the evaluation process and a multidisciplinary team must conduct a multi-faceted evaluation to determine whether the student is in need of special education services within a full continuum of alternative placement options.

TEN TIPS FOR TEACHERS

1. PBIS systems should be used as a prevention model.
2. All BIP should be based on a FBA.
3. Data collection and analysis of the information are critical components of the functional assessment.
4. All replacement behaviors should serve the same function as the target behavior.

5. Use an ABC analysis that has a scatter plot imbedded in the form.
6. Remember to have fidelity checks of all BIPs within your classroom.
7. Use a multi-assessment process when identifying children for E/BD (e.g., records reviews, observations, interviews, behavior rating scales).
8. Use appropriate behavior rating scales for assessment of E/BD based on the child's age and developmental level.
9. Write IEP goals for students with E/BD in the following areas: academic performance, adult and peer relationships, building and classroom expectations, vocational and reintegration.
10. Make placement decisions for students with E/BD based on their needs.

QUESTIONS FOR DISCUSSION

1. You have been asked by a teacher to observe in his classroom because he is having difficulty with Jordan. When you observe, what key points will you be looking for?
2. A behavior intervention plan was developed by the IEP team of which you were a part. The teacher is having difficulty following the behavior intervention plan. What might you suggest be done?
3. If you are part of the evaluation team for a student who has been referred because of acting out behaviors, and are going to conduct an interview with the parent, what questions will you ask the parent?

REFERENCES

Abgar, V. (1953). A proposal for a new method of evaluation of the newborn infant. *Current Researches in Anesthesia and Analgesia, 32,* 260–67.

Alberto, P. A., and Troutman, A. C. (2013). *Applied behavior analysis for teachers* (9th Ed.). Upper Saddle River, NJ: Merrill/Prentice Hall.

Baer, D. M., Wolf, M. M., and Risley, T. R. (1968). Some current dimensions of applied behavior analysis. *Journal of Applied Analysis, 1,* 91–97.

Beavers, G. A. and Iwata, B. A, (2011). Prevalence of multiply controlled probelm behavior. *Journal of Applied Behavior Analysis, 44(3),* 593–97.

Bijou, S. W., Peterson, R. F., and Ault, M. H. (1968). A method to integrate descriptive and experimental field studies at the level of data and empirical concepts. *Journal of Applied Behavioral Analysis, 1(2),* 175–91.

Carr, E. G., Levin, L., McConnachie, G., Carlson, J. L., Kemp, D. C., and Smith, C. E. (1994). *Communication-based intervention for problem behavior: A user's guide for producing positive behavior change.* Baltimore, MD: Paul H. Brookes.

Chandler, L. K., and Dahlquist, C. M. (2014). *Functional assessment: Strategies to prevent and remediate challenging behavior in school settings* (3rd Ed.). Upper Saddle River, NJ: Merrill/Prentice Hall.

Christner, R., Bolton, J., and Zarabba, J. (2011). *Anxiety disorders in the classroom: An action plan for identification, evaluation, and interventions.* Horsham, PA: LRP Publications.

Crone, D. A. and Horner, R. H. (2003). *Building positive behavior support systems in schools: Functional behavioral assessment.* New York: Guilford Press.

Desrochers, M. N. and Fallon, M. (2014). *Instruction in functional assessment.* Genesea, NY: Open SUNY Textbooks.

Dragsow, E. and Yell, M. L. (2001). Functional behavioral assessment: Legal requirements and challenges. *School Psychology Review, 30(2),* 239–51.

Durrand, V. M. and Crimmins, D. B. (1988). The Motivation Assessment Scale. *Journal of Autism and Developmental Disabilities, 18(1),* 99–117.

Gresham, F. M. (2000). Assessment of social skills in students with emotional behavioral disorders. *Assessment for Effective Intervention, 26(1),* 51–58.

Gresham, F. M., Lane, K., McIntyre, L. L., Olson-Tinker, H., Dolstra, L., and MacMillan, D. L., and Bocian, K. (2001). Risk factors associated with the co-occurence of hyper activity-impulsivity-inattention and conduct problems. *Behavioral Disorders, 26(3),* 189–99.

Gresham, F. M., MacMillan, D. L., and Bocian, K. (1996). Behavioral earthquakes: Low frequency, salient behavioral events that differentiate students at risk for behavioral disorders. *Behavioral Disorders, 21(4),* 277–92.

Individuals with Disabilities Improvement Act of 2004, PL 108–446, 20 U.S.C. §§ 1400 *et seq.*

Jones, V., Dohrn, E., and Dunn, C. (2004). *Creating effective programs for students with emotional and behavior disorders: Interdisciplinary approaches for adding meaning and hope to behavior change interventions.* Boston, MA: Pearson.

Jones, V., Greenwood, A., and Dunn, C. (2016). *Effective supports for students with emotional and behavioral disorders.* Upper Saddle River, NJ: Pearson.

Kauffman, J. M. and Landrum, T. J. (2013). *Characteristics of emotional and behavioral disorders of children and youth* (10th Ed.). Upper Saddle River, NJ: Pearson.

Keogh, B. and Speece, D. (1996). Learning disabilities within the context of schooling. In D. Speece and B. Keogh (Eds.), *Research on classroom ecologies: Implications of inclusion of children with learning disabilities* (pp. 1–14), Mahwah, NJ: Lawrence Erlbaum Associates.

Kern, L., O'Neill, R. E., and Starosta, K. (2005). Gathering functional assessment information. In L. M. Bombara and L. Kern (Eds.). *Individualized supports for students with problem behaviors: Designing positive behavior plans* (pp. 129–64). New York: Guilford Press.

Lane, K. L., Kalberg, L. J., and Menzies, H. M. (2009). *Developing school wide programs to prevent and manage problem behaviors.* New York: Guilford Press.

Lewis, T. J., Scott, T. M., and Sugai, G. M. (1994). The Problem Behavior Questionnaire: A teacher-based instrument to develop functional hypotheses of problem behavior in general education classrooms. *Diagnostique, 19,* 103–15.

Mayer, G. R. and McGookin, R. (1977). *Behavioral consulting.* Los Angeles, CA: Los Angeles County Superintendent of schools.

McConaughy, S. and Ritter, D. (2002). Best practices in multidimensional assessment of emotional and behavioral disorders. In A. Thomas and J. Grimes (Eds.), *Best practices in school psychology IV, 2,* 1303–20.

Merrell, K. (2008). *Behavioral, social, and emotional assessment of children and adolescents* (3rd Ed.). New York: Routledge.

Merrell, K. W. (1994). *Assessment of behavioral, social, and emotional problems: Direct and objective methods for use with children and adolescents.* White Plains, NY: Longman.

Miltenberger, R. G. (2012). *Behavior modification: Principles and procedures* (5th Ed.). Belmont, CA: Cengage.

Mueller, M. M., Nkosi, A., and Hine, J. F. (2011). Functional analysis in public schools: A summary of 90 functional analyses. *Journal of Applied Behavior Analysis, 44(4),* 807–18.

National Association of School Psychologists. (2005). *Position statement on students with emotional and behavioral disorders*. Bethesda, MD: Author.

O'Neill, R. E., Horner, R. H., Albin, R. W., Storey, K., and Sprague, J. R. (2015). *Functional analysis of problem behavior: A practical assessment guide* (3rd Ed). Pacific Grove, CA: Brookes/Cole.

Overton, T. (2009). *Assessing learners with special needs: An applied approach* (6th Ed.). Columbus, OH: Merrill/Prentice Hall.

Pierangelo, R. and Giulani, G. A. (2006). *Assessment in special education* (2nd Ed.). Boston, MA: Allyn & Bacon.

Power, T. and Eiraldi, R. (2000). Educational and psychiatric classification systems. In E. Shapiro and T. Kratochwill (Eds.) *Behavioral assessment in schools: Theory, research and clinical foundations* (pp. 464 –88). New York, NY: Guilford Press.

Reid, R. and Maag, J. (1994). How many fidgets in a pretty much: A critique of behavior rating scales for identifying students with ADHD. *Journal of School Psychology, 32,* 339–54.

Skinner, B. F. (1953). *The science of human behavior.* New York: Macmillan.

Tibbetts, T. J. (2013). *Identifying and assessing students with emotional disturbance.* Baltimore, MD: Paul H. Brookes.

Touchette, P. E., MacDonald, R. F., and Langer, S. N. (1985). Scatter plot for identifying stimulus control of problem behavior. *Journal of Applied Analysis, 18,* 343–52.

Walker, H. M. and Severson, H. H. (1990). *Systematic Screening for Behavior Disorders (SSBD): A multiple gating procedure.* Longmont, CO: Sopris West.

Walker, H. M., Severson, H. H., Nicholson, F., Kehle, T., Jenson, W. R. and Clark, E. (1994). Replication of the Systematic Screening for Behavior Disorders (SSBD): Procedure for the identification of at-risk children. *Journal of Emotional and Behavioral Disorders, 2,* 66–77.

Worthen, B., Borg, W., and White, K. (1993). *Measurement and evaluation in the schools: A practical guide.* New York: Longman.

Yell, M. L., Meadows, N. B., Drasgow, E., and Shiner, J. G. (2013). *Evidenced-based practices for educating students with emotional and behavioral disorders* (2nd Ed.). Upper Saddle River, NJ: Pearson.

3

SETTING UP YOUR CLASSROOM TO MEET BEHAVIORAL/EMOTIONAL CHALLENGES

Mr. Franciano is a new special education teacher recently hired in a school district to work with students with significant behavioral/emotional challenges. The previous teacher's contract was not renewed because she lacked control over her classroom. Her students were running up and down the halls and throwing items across the classroom. The principal had wanted the students to be integrated into regular classes, but this teacher did not want to work with the other teachers because she was overwhelmed with trying to keep order within her room. Mr. Franciano meets with the principal, who wants to be supportive of him, but is not sure how to deal with the class, especially after it has been out of control. Where does Mr. Franciano start? How does he meet the needs of the students? How does he work with the other teachers? Read on for what Mr. Franciano can do.

CEC INITIAL LEVEL SPECIAL EDUCATOR PREPARATION STANDARDS

2.0 Beginning special education professionals create safe, inclusive, culturally responsive learning environments so that individuals with exceptionalities become active and effective learners and develop emotional well-being, positive social interactions, and self-determination.

2.1 Beginning special education professionals through collaboration with general educators and other colleagues create safe, inclusive, culturally responsive learning environments to engage individuals with exceptionalities in meaningful learning activities and social interactions.

2.2 Beginning special education professionals use motivational and instructional interventions to teach individuals with exceptionalities how to adapt to different environments.

2.3 Beginning special education professionals know how to intervene safely and appropriately with individuals with exceptionalities in crisis.

5.0 Beginning special education professionals select, adapt, and use a repertoire of evidence-based instructional strategies to advance learning of individuals with exceptionalities.

5.1 Beginning special education professionals consider an individual's abilities, interests, learning environments, and cultural and linguistic factors in the selection, development, and adaptation of learning experiences for individuals with exceptionalities.

5.5 Beginning special education professionals develop and implement a variety of education and transition plans for individuals with exceptionalities across a wide range of settings and different learning experiences in collaboration with individuals, families, and teams.

CHAPTER OBJECTIVES

Readers will be able:

1. To articulate the differences between proactive and pre-corrective strategies and reactive and corrective strategies.
2. To describe at least five components of effective programs for students with emotional/behavioral disorders.
3. To describe five ways of arranging a classroom physically to promote learning and active engagement.
4. To describe five characteristics of positive classroom expectations.
5. To define five strategies for promoting a positive teacher-student relationship.

6. To articulate three strategies to transition students with emotional/behavioral disorders into general education settings.

KEY VOCABULARY TERMS

Physical environment—The classroom arrangement of furniture, computers, bulletin boards, projectors, and personal objects.

Seating arrangements—The arrangement of where the students sit which allows maximum supervision.

Positive classroom expectations—The rules established by the administration, teachers, and students where appropriate that define the expected behavior for students.

Reintegration—The process of moving students from instructional special education classes into general education settings.

KEY COMPONENTS OF EFFECTIVE E/BD PROGRAMS

There is no doubt that research provides a wide range of preventive and corrective methods for supporting students with emotional and behavioral disorders (Walker, Ramsey, and Gresham, 2004). These methods are infrequently implemented effectively to assist this population. Hill Walker and his colleagues (Walker et al., 1996) noted that:

> In most cases the failure to achieve meaningful outcomes is due to a poor match between presenting problems and the selected intervention, a less than adequate implementation of the intervention, lack of necessary resources, or a failure to treat the problem(s) comprehensively throughout the implementation process. . . . Frequently these intervention practices are sustained by unrealistic expectations about what is actually required to produce enduring changes in student behavior or by a natural tendency to quickly eliminate the immediate presenting problem rather than focus on the source. (p. 197)

These statements are supported by the research conducted by Knitzer, Steinberg, and Fleisch (1990). Based on their evaluations of programs serving students with emotional and behavioral disorders (E/BD) in the

United States, these researchers offer a negative description of programs for students with E/BD.

> Central to many of the classrooms that we visited was great concern with behavioral point systems. Yet often, these seemed largely designed to help maintain silence in the classroom, not to teach children how to better manage their anger, sadness, or impulses. . . . Although many of the children identified as behaviorally or emotionally handicapped under the law allegedly "lack social skills" the school day provides limited and sometimes only artificial opportunities (that is, thoroughly specialized curricula that are not integrated into the classroom) for them to master experiences of cooperating with peers. . . . In many programs. . . . There is limited, if any mental health presence. Children often lack access to therapy and teachers for consultation and support, even in the face of predictable crises. (pp. xii–xiii)

Programs for students with E/BD must be multifaceted and go far beyond behavior management and individualized behavior change plans. Twenty-four years later, we are still facing the same challenges and problems that Knitzer et al. (1990) documented in their research. No single strategy works with all students, consequently, teachers needs to be proficient in both proactive and pre-corrective strategies (antecedents) and reactive and corrective strategies (consequences) in addressing the academic and behavioral needs of their students (Yell, Meadows, Drasgow, and Shiner, 2013).

Teachers' experiences and researchers' extensive review of the literature has led to an understanding that there are key components that school personnel must attend to in order to provide comprehensive programming and effective interventions for students with E/BD (see Appendix C).

Physical Arrangement of the Classroom

Classroom organization helps ensure that activities in the classroom are stable and predictable for students. The level of organization sets the stage for learning and acceptable behavior. Proper classroom arrangement can affect student behavior in four ways: (a) can decrease student noise and disruption; (b) can eliminate inappropriate student exchanges; (c) increase desirable student interactions by use of centers around the room; and (d) increase the time students spend on academic tasks.

Researchers have examined the relationship between the classroom environment, student behavior, and academic engagement (Hood-Smith and Leffingwell, 1983; Vesser, 2001). A strategically organized classroom permits more positive interactions between teachers and students; reducing the probability that challenging behavior will occur (Martella, Nelson, and Marchand-Martella, 2003). Furthermore, adapting the classroom environment may serve as a direct intervention for children and youth who demonstrate ongoing disruptive behavior (Conroy, Davis, Fox, and Brown, 2002).

Environmental modifications are a preventative whole class approach that may decrease chronic challenging behaviors; prevent behavior problems for students who are at risk, and allow children with minimal or no problem behavior to access learning without interruption (Emmer and Stough, 2001). Although environmental modifications are a critical part of classroom management, many educators are not aware of the process of implementing those (Guardino and Fullerton, 2010).

Designing the Physical Environment

Strategically arranging the physical environment is a feasible starting point for developing classroom structure because all teachers face this task before the school year begins (Evertson and Emmer, 2009). Physical environment involves such items as furniture (e.g., teacher, paraprofessional, and student desks, bookcases, tables), computers, bulletin boards, projectors, and personal objects that teachers might want in their classrooms (plants, aquariums, classroom pets).

A logical classroom physical arrangement can facilitate student performance in three areas. First, thoughtful arrangements of the classroom can decrease student noise and disruption. Additionally, when student disruptions are decreased, on-task behavior and academic productivity often increases. Second, proper organization of classroom space can increase the level and quality of students' interactions (e.g., many times students with E/BD spend time talking to other students when they should be engaged academically). An efficient classroom environment can increase the teachers' proximity to their students. When teachers are in close proximity to students, they can ensure that students are doing the right things at the right time (Savage and Savage, 2010; Yell et al., 2013).

The fundamental rules regarding the physical setup of the classroom are that the room should be organized to (a) permit orderly movement, (b) keep distractions to a minimum, (c) make efficient use of available space, and (d) organize classroom space so that the students can attend to the teacher (Evertson and Emmer, 2009).

There are four keys to making decisions about classroom arrangements. First, high-traffic areas should be free of congestion. This is important because areas that are used frequently, such as pencil sharpener, water fountain, free-time area, and computer stations, can become locations of distractions and disruptions. These areas should be widely separated from each other, have adequate space, and be easy for students and the teacher to supervise and get to. Procedures should also be developed to regulate their use. Second, staff must be able to observe all students at all times.

Because monitoring of students' behavior is a critical task, clear lines of sight among instructional areas, teachers and students' desks, and student work areas must be maintained. Evertson and Emmer (2009) recommend that when arranging their classrooms, teachers should stand in different locations of the room and check for blind spots. Third, materials that are frequently used by staff and students should be readily available. This will ensure lessons transitioning smoothly because materials will be readily at hand.

Fourth, the students' seating arrangements should allow them to see lessons without moving their desks. This will enhance the opportunity for students to be involved in the lesson (Emmer and Evertson, 2009; Evertson and Emmer, 2009; Yell et al., 2013).

Walker and colleagues (2004) recommended, prior to organizing the physical environment, a teacher should identify all functions and activities that will take place during the school day and carefully organize the room to accomplish these functions. They suggest the following functions and arrangements: (a) an independent work area consisting of individual students' desks in low-traffic areas and away from materials, time-out areas, and free activity centers; (b) a small group work area where distractions are at a minimum and students can focus to each other and other students; (c) a free time or choice activity area in a quiet location of the classroom for students who finish their work early or earn reinforcers; (d) a time-out or penalty area that isolates misbehaving students in a corner or the back of the classroom; (e) a quiet time area that can be utilized to calm an agitated student, and (f) the teacher's desk, which should be located in a low traffic area and out of the way so it receives as little use as possible during instruction.

An appropriate placement for a teacher's desk is in the front corner of the room facing the students. The paraprofessional's desk could be placed in a back corner opposite the teacher's desk (Yell et al., 2013). Possible masking tape should border the teacher's and paraprofessionals desks to indicate an off-limits area for students. To maintain student desk area, tape can also be placed around the students' desks.

Walker et al. (2004) also suggested organizing the classroom with a notice board announcing activities, projects, and recognitions, placed in highly visible areas, and storage areas located in low-traffic areas to ensure easy access and to avoid distractions. If a teacher utilizes different areas in the classroom for various functions (e.g., free-time area, time-out area, cool-down area, computer area) they should identify the boundaries for each of these areas.

Setting Up Classroom Seating Arrangements

Several researchers have reported that the closer staff are in relation to their students, often referred to as proximity control, (a) the greater the control of their interactions with other students, (b) the higher the rates of on-task behavior, and (c) the lower the rates of student disruption (Gunter, Shores, Jack Rasmussen, and Flowers, 1995).

Etsheidt, Stainback, and Stainback (1984) reported that for proximity control to be most effective, the staff must be within about three feet of a student. The empirical evidence subsequently indicates that staff should circulate around their classrooms and make frequent individual interactions with their students (to either use effective praise or corrective teaching).

Smith and Yell (2013) cautioned against placing potentially disruptive students close in proximity of each other and suggested that the potentially problematic students should be seated next to students who exhibit appropriate behavior.

When determining student seating, teachers should implement a flexible approach to seating arrangements to accommodate the various learning functions that occur in the classroom (Smith and Yell, 2013). Student desks should not face sources of distraction (e.g., window, free time areas). There should be enough room around each desk so that the staff can circulate and work individually with the students. Therefore, allowing the students to attend to lessons, individual seatwork is facilitated, and teachers can move freely around the classroom, consequently allowing staff to monitor student behavior (Yell et al., 2013).

When teachers set up their classrooms in the traditional row style for lectures, presentations, and demonstration, they may encounter that this arrangement is less appropriate for small group work. Teachers may choose to use small tables for these activities. When staffs are teaching in small group areas, they should face the rest of the class (Yell ct al., 2013). See Appendix C for guidelines for setting up the physical environment for your classroom.

CLASSROOM EXPECTATIONS

Good and Brophy (2008) elaborated on a consensus in the literature that "teachers expectations can and sometimes do affect teacher-student inter-action and student outcome" (p. 81). High teacher expectations for students' behavior and academic performance have been consistently iden-tified as a key correlate of effective schools (Walker et al., 2004). Teach-ers should strive to maintain flexible expectations and emphasize the positive.

Teachers should develop and project expectations that are as positive as possible, while still being realistic. Good and Brophy (2008) suggested that teachers should: (a) highlight positive achievements and behaviors of students, (b) keep expectations up-to-date by monitoring student progress, (c) set goals for classes and individual students in terms of acceptable standards vs. unacceptable standards and let progress deter-mine educational and behavioral programming, (d) stress students' con-tinuous progress relative to their previous levels rather than comparing them to other students when giving feedback, (e) provide feedback that will help students meet their academic and behavioral objectives, and (f) encourage students to achieve and behave as much as they can.

When posting and sharing classroom expectations, the expectations should be few in number, positive, easy to understand, and accompanied by pictures or photos (Johns, 2018). Teachers must teach the expectations and reinforce those students who follow the expectations. These expectations should be reviewed and re-taught periodically, especially after school vacations.

Positive Teacher-Student Relationship

It is critical that teachers, who attempt to build strong positive relationships with students with E/BD, be persistent, consistent, and predictable in their own behavior. Therefore, they must look for positive attributes in students that can be used as the foundation for fostering a positive relationship. When students and teachers have a positive relationship and students know that they are liked and respected, they are more likely to emulate the teacher's behavior, have better attitudes concerning school, and have higher levels of academic achievement (Good and Brophy, 2008; Smith and Yell, 2013).

Developing a consistent classroom structure is another avenue to build a positive classroom climate. Structure means the manner in which teachers organize their classrooms to ensure that teaching and learning are enhanced and problem behavior are minimized (Yell et al., 2013). The central goal, when developing a classroom structure, is to ensure that events in the classroom are structured and predicable (Walker et al., 2004). Teachers that establish classrooms that are structured and predicable find a reduction in problem behaviors, while the likelihood of effective learning is increased (Darch and Kame'enui, 2004; Good and Brophy, 2008; Walker et al., 2004).

Maintaining a Positive Classroom Climate

In a study, conducted in twenty-eight third-grade classrooms, researchers found that the smooth and automatic functioning of classrooms of effective classroom managers was the consequence of careful planning, preparation, and organization at the beginning of the school year (Evertson and Emmer, 2009).

The most effective teachers spent a good deal of time on instructing about the operation of the classroom, including their expectations for behavior, routines, and classroom rules. Additionally, effective classroom managers described the operation of the classroom, modeled correct procedures, answered questions, and had students practice and receive feedback regarding procedures, rules, and consequences (Evertson and Emmer, 2009).

Comparable studies conducted in junior high schools demonstrated similar findings (Evertson and Emmer, 2009). In well-managed classrooms, teachers have clear ideas of what types of classroom circumstances and student behaviors a healthy learning environment necessitates (Evertson and Emmer, 2009).

PREPARING FOR TRANSITIONS WITHIN THE CLASSROOM

Students with emotional/behavioral disorders often have difficulty moving from one activity to another. It may stress them to make a change. They may be comfortable with what they are doing and don't want to move to another activity. They may be in the middle of doing something and don't want to quit. Children with emotional/behavioral disorders need to be prepared for changes.

The teacher may want to create a verbal and visual cue when there is five minutes left of an activity and time to pick up what they are doing and put the materials away. There are a number of timer systems that assist teachers in giving those visual cues. When students start putting items away, they should be reinforced for preparing for a new activity. There may be another one-minute signal that time is almost up. Again, that signal should be visual and verbal and those students who put items away should be recognized.

PREPARING FOR TRANSITIONS TO OTHER CLASSROOMS

The reintegration of students with E/BD, into general education settings, is one of the most important components of effective E/BD programs. Unfortunately, it is one of the weakest links of programming for students with E/BD at any level (elementary, junior-high, high schools) (Callahan et al., 1993; Huntz and Werner, 1982). The reintegration of students with E/BD into integrated settings requires careful and systematic individualized planning. It requires collaborative planning between general educators and special educators.

Several experts in the field of E/BD have suggested that effective integration of students into general education settings be contingent on methodology and policies that are based on scientific evidence (Simpson, 2004; Wood, 2002; Zionts, 1997). Consequently, it could be argued that one explanation for the relatively poor outcomes experienced by many students with E/BD who are educated in general education settings either by reintegration or inclusion is that such evidence has been notably lacking and has not been the foundation for implementing reintegration and inclusive policies (Lewis, Chard, and Scott, 1994; Loeber and Farmington, 2001; U. S. Department of Education, 2003).

Despite the critical importance of implementing appropriate reintegration practices, research reports very little success in the return of students with E/BD into regular education settings (Callahan et al., 1993; Gable, Hendrickson, and Algozzine, 1987; Osborne, Shulte, and McKinney, 1991). In fact, it has been reported that less than 10 percent of students with E/BD ever return permanently to an integrated setting (Steinberg and Knitzer, 1992).

Disturbing data also indicate that many special education teachers fail to attempt to reintegrate their students with E/BD into integrated settings (Callahan et al., 1993). Laycock and Tonelson (1985) reported that over two-thirds of the teachers surveyed reintegrated a total of five or fewer students during the previous three years. When special education teachers do try to reintegrate students, learning and behavior problems success rates are as low as 12 to 33 percent (Gable et al., 1987; Osborne et al., 1991).

When students with E/BD remain in inclusive settings following reintegration attempts, very few perform at successful academic levels (Osborne et al., 1991). There appears to be a critical need for the development and implementation of systematic, empirically demonstrated reintegration models which will target and alleviate some of the factors resulting in poor reintegration success rates among students with E/BD (Gable et al., 1987; Laycock and Tonelson, 1985).

Problems in the Reintegration of Students with E/BD

Factors that impact the success or failure of reintegration fall into three broad categories: (a) teacher and student factors; (b) programming factors; and (c) physical/ environmental factors (Callahan et al., 1993). The components making up each of these categories will be discussed now.

Teacher and Student Factors

A possible reason for the poor rates of successful reintegration of students with E/BD may include a variety of teacher and student factors. Foremost among these factors are the attitudes and expectations of regular education teachers toward students with E/BD, which ultimately may impact the teachers' willingness to receive these students into their classrooms (Callahan et al., 1993).

Another factor may be the lack of training pre-service teachers receive. A third factor may be the anxiety and fear teachers might have in managing the student with E/BD's challenging behavior. However, according to researchers, challenging classroom behavior may be a function of ineffective instruction rather than the presence of students with E/BD within the classroom (Yell et al., 2013). A final factor that contributes to reintegration problems is the reported widespread lack of communication and consultation between the regular and special education teacher (Callahan et al., 1993; Osborne et al., 1991).

Programming Factors

Many of the reintegration problems, related to a specific classroom, may be due to a lack of planning by the special education teacher for the eventuality of reintegration (Callahan et al., 1993). In addition, it has been reported that special education teachers fail to implement essential steps in a comprehensive reintegration program (Gable, Laycock, Maroney, and Smith, 1991).

Fundamental to this problem is the lack of a systematic, written plan to guide initial reintegration efforts, and the lack of subsequent ongoing evaluation and assessment throughout the reintegration process (Callahan et al., 1993). According to Gable and Laycock (1991), approximately 50 percent of all school districts have a written policy governing reintegration.

> This absence of uniform practice invites inconsistent and arbitrary decision-making and seriously impedes the mainstream process. (p. 4)

Physical/Environmental Factors

Constraints of regular education teachers, large class size, and unavailability of support services often negatively impact a regular education teachers' willingness to accept students with disabilities into their classroom (Callahan et al., 1993). Huntz and Werner (1982) listed the physical setting (e.g., the physical layout of the school building and receiving classroom) as a critical area to consider when creating a match between the special education student and the regular education classroom environment.

Guidelines for Successful Reintegration

Due to a lack of literature, detailing how to successfully conduct reintegration programs for students with E/BD, Callahan et al. (1993) reviewed the available literature on reintegration, synthesized common components of model reintegration programs, and through their many years of classroom experience with students with E/BD, developed guidelines for the reintegration of E/BD students into integrated settings.

These guidelines consist of strategies which could be used by teachers, administrators, and individual education plan (IEP) teams to facilitate a four-step reintegration process for students with E/BD, which include the following components: (a) long-range planning and preparation; (b) immediate preparation for reintegration; (c) initiating reintegration; and follow up and evaluation. Appendix E will outline these guidelines. These guidelines can be modified to suit the needs of individual teachers and school districts. Additionally, no timelines have been recommended because the authors acknowledge that the strategies will take varying lengths of time for each individual student.

For a variety of reasons, the reintegration of students with E/BD, despite the critical importance within the overall scope of special education programming, rarely is successful or effective. Many of the problems and obstacles encountered by special educators in their reintegration practices, such as negative attitudes and expectations by regular educators, a lack of communication and collaboration, and demanding program requirements, present serious challenges to the perseverance, creativity, and commitment of teachers of students with E/BD.

IN SUMMARY

Planning ahead to design your classroom is critical in meeting the needs of your students with behavioral/emotional challenges. You must establish a method for how you want your classroom to look, decide the expectations for your students, and look ahead to plan for opportunities for students to interact with their classroom peers.

TEN TIPS FOR TEACHERS

1. Develop a proactive management style (e.g., use of proximity control, use of pre-correction, teacher expectations, develop positive relationships with students, etc.).
2. Promote and practice consistency and structure on an ongoing basis in your classroom.
3. Prior to organizing the physical space in your classroom identify and determine all the functions that will go on in your classroom (e.g., social skills instruction, small group instruction, large group instruction, free time, computer center, etc.).
4. Ensure high traffic areas are free of congestion.
5. Make sure the classroom space is organized in such a way that you can observe all students at all times.
6. Separate potentially problematic students away from each other.
7. Teach your classroom and school expectations to students on the first day of school.
8. Look for positive attributes in your students that can be used to foster positive relationships.
9. Assess the integrated setting before integrating your students into a regular education classroom.
10. Communicate with the regular education teacher in which you have your student(s) integrated into on a consistent and regular basis.

QUESTIONS FOR DISCUSSION

1. Which of the components of an effective program for E/BD students do you believe is the most important and why?
2. You are slowly and systematically integrating a student and have prepared him for a general education class full time. You decide to have a new IEP to discuss the possibility. The student's behavior regresses and he increases his aggressive behavior. You think he may be afraid to return full time. What will you add to the plan to support him?
3. What are five components of an effective E/BD program?

REFERENCES

Callahan, K. J., Gustafson, K., and Cancio, E. J. (1993). Guidelines for the successful reintegration of students with emotional and behavioral disorders. In R. B. Rutherford, Jr. and S. R. Mathur (Eds.), *Monograph in behavioral disorders: Severe behavior disorders of children and youth* (pp. 55–63). Reston, VA: Council for Children with Behavioral Disorders of the Council for Exceptional Children.

Conroy, M. A., Davis, C. A., Fox, J. J., and Brown, W. H. (2002). Functional assessment of behavior and effective supports of young children with challenging behaviors. *Assessment for Effective Intervention, 27(4)*, 35–47.

Darch, C. B., and Kame'enui, E. J. (2004). *Instructional classroom management: A proactive approach to behavior management* (2nd Ed.). Upper Saddle River, NJ: Merrill/Prentice Hall.

Emmer, E. T., and Evertson, C. M. (2009). *Classroom management for middle and high school teachers* (8th Ed.). Upper Saddle River, NJ: Pearson/Merrill Education.

Emmer, E. T., and Stough, L. M. (2001). Classroom management: A critical part of educational psychology and teacher education. *Educational Psychologist, 36,* 103–12.

Etsheidt, S., Stainback, S., and Stainback, W. (1984). The effectiveness of teacher proximity as an initial technique of helping pupils control their behavior. *The Pointer, 28,* 33–35.

Evertson, C. M., and Emmer, E. T. (2009). *Classroom management for elementary teachers* (8th Ed.). Upper Saddle River, NJ: Pearson/Merrill Education.

Gable, R. A., Hendrickson, J. M., and Algozzine, B. (1987). *Correlates of successful mainstreaming of behaviorally disordered adolescents.* In S. Braaten, R. B. Rutherford Jr., and J. Maag (Eds.), *Programming for adolescents with behavioral disorders* (v. 3, pp. 16–26) Reston, VA: Council for Children with Behavioral Disorders.

Gable, R. A., Laycock, V. K. (1991). Part I: Organizational and administrative aspects of regular classroom integration. In R. A. Gable, V. K. Laycock, S. A. Maroney, and C. R. Smith (Eds.), *Programming to integrate students with behaviorally disorders* (pp. 4–14). Reston, VA: Council for Exceptional Children.

Gable, R. A., Laycock, V. K., Maroney, S. A., and Smith, C. R. (1991). *Preparing to integrate students with behavioral disorders* (Eds.). Reston, VA: Council for Exceptional Children.

Good, T. L., and Brophy, J. E. (2008). *Looking in classrooms* (10th Ed.). Boston, MA: Pearson/ Allyn and Bacon.

Guardino, C. A., and Fullerton, E. (2010). Changing behaviors by changing the classroom environment. *Teaching Exceptional Children, 42(6),* 8–13.

Gunter, P. L., Shores, R. E., Jack, S. L., Rasmussen, S. K., and Flowers, J. (1995). On the move: Using teacher proximity to improve students' behavior. *Teaching Exceptional Children, 28*, 12–14.

Hood-Smith, N. E., and Leffingwell, R. J. (1983). The impact of physical space alternation on disruptive classroom behavior: A case study. *Education, 104*, 224–31.

Huntz, S. L., and Werner, R. J. (1982). *Monograph 4: Reintegrating behaviorally disordered students into general education classroom.* Des Moines, IA: Drake University, Midwest Regional Resource Center (ERIC Document Reproduction Service No Ed 231, 113).

Knitzer, J., Steinberg, Z., and Fleisch, B. (1990). *At the schoolhouse door: An examination of programs and policies for children with behavioral and emotional problems.* New York: Bank Street College of Education.

Laycock, V. K., and Tonelson, S. W. (1985). Preparing emotionally disturbed adolescents for the mainstream: An analysis of current practices. In S. Braaten, R. B. Rutherford, Jr., and W. Evan (Eds.), *Programming for adolescents with behavioral disorders* (vol. 2), pp. 63–73. Reston, VA: Council for Children with Behavioral Disorders.

Lewis, T. J., Chard, D., and Scott, T. M. (1994). Full inclusion and the education of children and youth with emotional and behavioral disorders. *Behavioral Disorders, 19(4)*, 277–93.

Loeber, R., and Farmington, D. (2001). *Serious juvenile offenders: Risk factors and successful interventions.* Thousand Oaks, CA: Sage Publications Group.

Martella, R. C., Nelson, J. R., and Marchand-Martella, N. E. (2003). *Managing disruptive behaviors in schools.* Boston, MA: Allyn and Bacon.

Osborne, S. S., Shulte, A. C., and McKinney, J. D. (1991). *A longitudinal study of students with learning disabilities in mainstream and resource programs. Exceptionality, 2(2)*, 81–95.

Savage, T. V., and Savage, M. K. (2010). *Successful classroom management and discipline: Teaching self-control and responsibility* (3rd Ed.). Thousand Oaks, CA: Sage.

Simpson, R. L. (2004). Inclusion of students with behavioral disorders in general education settings: Research and measurement issues. *Behavioral Disorders, 30*(1), 19–31.

Smith, S. W., and Yell, M. L. (2013). A teacher's guide to preventing problem behaviors in elementary classrooms. Upper Saddle River, NJ: Pearson/Merrill Education.

Steinberg, Z., and Knitzer, J. (1992). Classrooms for emotionally and behaviorally disturbed students: Facing the challenge. *Behavioral Disorders, 17*, 145–56.

U. S. Department of Education (2003). *Twenty-fifth report to Congress on implementation of the Individuals with Disabilities Education Act.* Washington, DC: Author.

Visser, J. (2001). Aspects of physical provision for pupils with emotional and behavioral difficulties. *Support for Learning, 16(2)*, 64–68.

Walker, H., Horner, R., Sugai, G., Bullis, M., Sprague, J., and Bricker, D. (1996). Integrated approaches to preventing antisocial behavior patterns among school-aged children and youth. *Journal of Emotional and Behavioral Disorders, 4*, 194–209.

Walker, H. M., Ramsey, E., and Gresham, F. M. (2004). *Antisocial behavior in the school: Evidence-based practices* (2nd Ed.). Belmont, CA: Thomson/Wadsworth.

Weinstein, C. S. (1979). The physical environment of the school: A review of research. *Review of Educational Research, 49*, 577–610.

Wood, J. W. (2002). *Adapting instruction to accommodate students in inclusive settings.* Upper Saddle River, NJ: Merrill/Prentice Hall.

Yell, M. L., Meadows, N. B., Drasgow, E., and Shiner, J. G. (2013). *Evidence-based practices for educating students with emotional and behavioral disorders* (2nd Ed.). Upper Saddle River, NJ: Pearson.

Zionts, P. (1997). Inclusion strategies for students with learning and behavior problems. Austin, TX: Pro-Ed.

4

BUILDING RELATIONSHIPS WITH CHILDREN AND YOUTH

Joe is a student who attends Springfield Middle School. He has been diagnosed with E/BD. He has been in an /EBD self-contained program since third grade. He has attended many schools and has struggled in every program he has been placed in since third grade. At Springfield Middle School there are two E/BD self-contained units. Joe has been placed in Mrs. Butke's E/BD classroom since sixth grade. Joe is in eighth grade and is going to the high school at the end of the year and continues to struggle in Mrs. Butke's classroom. Mr. Clark, Mr. Knowlton's E/BD supervisor, tells him he is going to transfer Joe into his classroom after Christmas break. Mr. Clark tells Mr. Knowlton that he feels Joe will be more successful in his classroom. What can Mr. Knowlton do to develop a strong positive student-teacher relationship with Joe?

STANDARDS

Council for Exceptional Children Initial Preparation Standard 1.0—
Beginning special education professionals understand how exceptionalities may interact with development and learning and use this knowledge to provide meaningful and challenging learning experiences for individuals with exceptionalities.
Council for Exceptional Children Initial Preparation Standard 2.0—
Beginning special education professionals create safe, inclusive,

culturally responsive learning environments so that individuals with exceptionalities become active and effective learners and develop emotional well being, positive social interactions, and self-determination.

CHAPTER OBJECTIVES

Readers will be able:

1. To articulate five reasons positive relationships are important when working with students with emotional/behavioral challenges.
2. To understand the teacher behaviors that students value.
3. To articulate the strategies that teachers can implement to build positive relationships.
4. To list five strategies that teachers can utilize to communicate effectively.

KEY TERMS

Positive Reinforcement—Presentation of a positive reinforcer (reward) contingent upon a behavior, which increases the probability that the behavior will be repeated.

Punishment—Consequences that reduce future probability of a behavior. May be response cost (removal of a valued object or commodity) or aversive conditioning (presentation of an aversive stimulus such as a slap or a revocation of privileges).

Response Cost—Punishment technique consisting of taking away a valued object or commodity contingent on a behavior (a fine). Making an inappropriate response "cost" something to the misbehaving child.

Positive Statements—Statements that are received positively by the student.

Negative Statements—Some form of teacher dissatisfaction or frustration with the student's work or behavior, redirections stated in a sharp and critical manner, or use of sarcasm.

Fixed Schedule of Reinforcement—Delivery of reinforcement on a constant basis. Either the number of times or average number of times the behavior occurs.

Positive Student-Teacher Relationships—In order for students to trust adults and eventually to view them as realistic models for appropriate behavior, it is crucial that adults develop positive relationships with students. This can be done be having numerous positive interactions by caregivers toward students.

High Expectations—Refers to any effort to set the same high educational standards for all students in the class, school, or educational system. Students who are expected to learn more or perform better generally do so, while those held to lower expectations usually achieve less.

Corrective Teaching—Corrective Teaching is an effective way to constructively respond to a child's misbehavior. You can use this method in many situations where you want to "correct" the child's challenging behavior.

Trauma—Trauma is a type of damage to the mind that occurs as a result of a severely distressing event. Trauma is often the result of an overwhelming amount of stress that exceeds one's ability to cope, or integrate the emotions involved with that experience.

Prosocial Behavior—Behavior that facilitates positive social contacts. Desirable or appropriate social behavior.

THE IMPORTANCE OF POSITIVE ADULT/STUDENT RELATIONSHIPS

When children feel threatened, it is difficult for them to make connections with their teachers. In order to build relationships, a non-threatening teacher and environment is critical for students. The brain is wired to minimize social stress and to maximize opportunities to connect. Most educators and parents agree that relationships affect children and youth's welfare. A growing body of research indicates why relationships matter in school and promoting high-quality relationships with children and youth is the best response to problem behaviors (Jones, Bailey, Brion-Meiesels, and Partee, 2016).

For example, research demonstrates that young children who experience warmth, trusting teacher-student relationships with low degree of conflict are more likely to have a positive adjustment to school (Rimm-Kaufman and Hamre, 2010) to perform well academically, and to have less behavior problems (Birch and Ladd, 1997; Ladd, Birch, and Buhs, 1999). These effects can be long lasting.

An investigation by Hamre and Pianta (2001) found that students with a strong positive relationship with their 1st grade teacher received better grades than their peers, even after accounting for differences in verbal ability and behavior problems. These academic gains continued across the elementary and middle school years. According to the same study, teacher-student relationships characterized by a high degree of conflict were associated with poor academic outcomes and behavior problems, including school avoidance and cooperation, lower classroom participation and increased peer-directed aggression.

Teachers who build positive relationships with students validate students' emotional experiences and promote a sense of security and belonging that supports their active engagement (Hugues, Luo, Kwok, and Loyd, 2008). In addition, high-quality relationships serve as protective factors during times of distress; these relationships are considered the "active ingredient" in building resilience among students who are "at-risk for academic problems or other poor development outcomes" (Center on the Developing Child at Harvard University, 2015; Meehan, Hughes, and Cavell, 2003).

A positive relationship with a supportive adult can buffer children and youth from trauma and other negative life experiences and can provide the personalized responsiveness and scaffolding necessary for adaptive skill building in the face of disruptive or challenging life events (Burchinal, Peisner-Feinberg, Pianta, and Howes, 2002). Not only do classrooms characterized by positive relationships better support social-emotional development in children, but the social-emotional competence of children and adults also influences the development of classroom relationships (Jones et al., 2016).

THE IMPORTANCE OF POSITIVE ADULT/STUDENT RELATIONSHIPS

Professionals in the field of emotional and behavior disorders (E/BD) have stated the importance of teacher-student relationships:

> [E]ducators who work with children and youth with E/BD make their most significant and enduring positive progress when they are able to forge trusting and positive relationships with their students and . . . interlinking these affirmative interpersonal relationships with effective methods. . . . [It] is only through constructive relationship formation that a method of curricula, independent of how allegedly effective it is, will have the potential to work most effectively. (Simpson, Peterson, and Smith, 2001, pp. 230–31)

Given the trauma experienced by many students who are identified as E/BD, it is not surprising that the development of positive teacher-relationships is a focal point of classrooms and schools concentrated on reducing the negative impact trauma has on students' school success (Birnamen and Page, 2012; Dods, 2013; Wright, 2013).

Based on a meta-analysis of more than 100 studies, Marzano, Marzano, and Pickering (2003) reported that positive student relationships were the basis of effective classroom management and that these positive relationships could reduce behavior problems by 31 percent. Gregory and Ripski (2008) found that teachers who reported that they used a relational approach were more likely to have students who demonstrated less defiant behavior than those teachers who did not report using such a style.

A study of interventions for students at-risk for serious behavior problems found that "the teacher-student relationship had more impact on students' behavior outcomes, academic competencies and school engagement" (Tsai and Cheney, 2012, p. 105).

The quality of teacher-student/adult-student relationships has also been shown to have an impact on adolescents' connectedness to schools and subsequent behavior problems and dropout status (Catalano et al., 2004), social skills (Pianta and Stuhlman, 2004), and the effectiveness of behavior interventions (Cheney et al., 2009; Crone, Hawken, and Horner, 2010).

James Kauffman (1997) noted that "teachers must listen, talk, and act in ways that communicate respect, caring, and confidence, both in themselves and their students" (p. 519). Teachers of students with E/BD list the quality of their relationship with students and their ability to effectively respond to student challenging behaviors as major factors impacting their job satisfaction and their decision to remain in teaching (Nelson, Maculan, Roberts, and Ohlund, 2011).

It is critical to note that research suggests students identified as E/BD have less positive and supportive interactions with their teachers than many other students (Jones, Greenwood, and Dunn, 2016). When receiving their education in inclusive classrooms, "these students receive less instruction, fewer instances of teacher praise and fewer opportunities to respond" (Scott, Alter, and Hirn, 2011, p. 620).

William Morse one of our pioneers of the field of E/BD writing with colleagues summarized how critical adult-student relationships are:

> Although there is no one solution to the multifaceted issue of effectively educating children and adolescents with E/BD, an important step that schools can take is to create a school climate that values and emphasizes caring. (Mihalas, Morse, Allsop, and McHattan, 2009, p. 110)

WHAT DO STUDENT SAY THEY VALUE IN TEACHERS?

Students' statements pertaining to effective teachers mirror those supported by research on effective teachers (Jones et al., 2016). "When I have asked students in interviews what makes a particular teacher 'special' and worthy of respect, the students consistently cite three characteristics: firmness, compassion, and an interesting, engaging, and challenging teaching style" (Noguera, 1995, p. 205).

Interviews conducted over a three-year period with 400 inner-city middle and high school students in Philadelphia present similar results (Corbett and Wilson, 2002). These students indicated that good teachers:

- made sure that students did their work
- controlled the classroom
- set limits
- were willing to assist students whenever and however they wanted help
- explained assignment and content clearly

- varied the classroom routine
- took time to get to know the students and their circumstances
- made learning fun (p. 18)

Based on a comprehensive review of the literature, Woolfolk and Weinstein (2006) found that students favored and responded most positively to teachers who possessed three sets of skills: (1) establishing caring relationships with students; (2) setting limits and creating a safe environment without being rigid, threatening, or punitive; and (3) making learning fun.

DEVELOPING POSITIVE RELATIONSHIPS WITH STUDENTS

In order for students to begin to trust adults and eventually view them as realistic models for appropriate behavior, it is critical that adults develop positive relationships with students identified as E/BD (Jones et al., 2016).

Another example that demonstrates why positive relationships with students are important is to relate it to a bank account. Unless one makes ample deposits in advance, it is not possible to make withdrawals when needed. If we have not made multiple deposits into a positive relationship "bank account," students with E/BD will not be willing to respond positively to our requests (Sutherland, Wehby, and Copeland, 2000). Research indicates that increased positive teacher behavior is associated with decreases in inappropriate student behavior (Shores and Wehby, 1999).

Teachers can also better understand their students and create a positive relationship "bank account" by taking an interest in what their students find interesting (Bondy, Ross, Gallingane, and Hambacher, 2017; Dunn, 2010). If students participate in any type of activity (either inside or outside school), teachers can make positive connections with students (and often their caregivers) by attending an event in which the student is involved (Jones et al., 2016). In a study conducted by Wilner, Kirigin, Braukmann, and Wolf (1997) they identified behaviors that validate social behaviors preferred by students.

METHODS FOR DEVELOPING POSITIVE TEACHER-STUDENT RELATIONSHIPS

There are numerous methods teachers can use to get to know students and ensure their students know they care about them as individuals. The following are methods to develop relationships with students:

- Stand by your classroom door and greet your students as they walk through the door.
- Arranging individual conferences with students.
- Demonstrating an interest in students' activities.
- Eating lunch with students.
- Having discussions with students in the hallway and at recess.
- Sending letters and notes to students.
- Using a suggestion box.
- Joining in school and community activities.
- Joining in on playground activities.
- Showing support for student diversity (Jones et al., 2016).

COMMUNICATING OPENLY AND HONESTLY WITH STUDENTS

Adults who work with students with E/BD can help them develop greater sensitivity to others by communicating openly and honestly with them. Most adolescents appreciate being treated with respect during private expressions of concern (Jones et al., 2016). Many students benefit from the experience of teachers who share some aspects of their lives that help students better understand the human condition. However, teachers need to avoid too much distance or too much familiarity. It is crucial that students understand we care about them while at the same time there being no confusion regarding the role the teacher serves.

A teacher is a model, mentor, teacher, counselor, and advocate, not a parent substitute, a personal friend, or buddy. It is crucial that students with E/BD perceive educators as individuals who are comfortable with themselves, who are emotionally stable; who have interests and relationships that the students can use as models (Jones et al., 2016).

MAINTAINING A HIGH RATE OF POSITIVE STATEMENTS AND LIMITING NEGATIVE STATEMENTS

We describe positive statements as those that are received positively by students. They typically involve statements reinforcing or encouraging students' academic work and social behavior or signifying to the students that the teacher knows them and values them as individuals. Negative statements typically involve some form of teacher disappointment or frustration with the students' work or behavior, redirections stated in a sharp and critical manner, or the use of sarcasm.

Corrections to students' academic work or behavior can, consequently, be either positive or negative dependent on the degree to which they are implemented in a positive and supportive manner (Jones et al., 2016).

A number of studies indicates that teachers in classrooms of students with E/BD have the vast majority of interactions with students following negative student behavior (Shores, Gunther, and Jack, 1993; Van Acker, Grant, and Henry, 1996). Shores and Wehby (1999) indicate "that the research has been consistent in its reports of (a) low rates of positive interactions between students with E/BD and their teachers and (b) the inconsistent nature of these interactions" (pp. 196–97).

According to Van Acker et al. (1996) these negative interactions are regrettable, because we have known for decades that high rates of teacher attention to prosocial student behavior is associated with improved behavior and performance. Gunter and his colleagues (1994) indicated that "when teacher praise rate was increased or when the method of decreasing commands changed, the aversive behaviors of the students did in fact decrease; negative interactions decreased, and positive interactions increased" (p. 36).

Research shows that having teachers provide students with attention on a fixed-time schedule (e.g., every fifteen minutes) can have a positive influence on student social behavior (Austin and Soeda, 2008; Riley, Mckevitt, Shriver, and Allen, 2011). Given the low rates of positive teacher attention to students identified as E/BD, it is possible that a fixed reinforcement schedule can significantly increase the amount of interactions students have with teachers, and particularly the number of times the teacher provides the student with positive feedback (Cancio and Johnson, 2013; Cancio and Johnson, 2007).

Research also indicates that when teachers increase their rate of specific positive feedback three positive things happen: (1) there is a decrease in disruptive student behavior, (2) the number of negative statements teachers make to students diminishes (Musti-Rao and Haydon, 2011), and (3) there is an increase in students' on-task behavior (Allday et al., 2012).

O'Leary and O'Leary (1977) stated that to serve as an effective reinforcer, feedback must have three qualities:

1. Contingency. Praise must immediately follow desired behaviors.
2. Specificity. Praise should describe the specific behaviors being reinforced (e.g., "Thanks for giving me eye contact when we were talking about showing your work on your math assignment").
3. Credibility. Praise is typically effective when it is appropriate for the situation and the individual.

COMMUNICATING HIGH EXPECTATIONS

Our expectations of student behavior are impacted by a variety of factors other than actual performance or behavior. Cook, Tankersley, Cook, and Landrum (2000) reported that teachers had more negative attitudes about students with disabilities who were included in their regular education classrooms. Teachers are obviously influenced by how students are identified (e.g., LD, E/BD, ID) and how they present themselves, as well as how they behave. Cooper and Good (1983) developed this list of common ways in which teachers respond differently to high-achieving students versus low-achieving students:

1. Seating low-expectation students far away from the teacher or seating them in a group
2. Paying less attention to low-achieving students in academic situations (i. e., smiling less often, maintaining less eye contact)
3. Calling less often on low-achieving students to answer classroom questions or to make public demonstrations
4. Waiting less time for low-expectation students to respond to questions

5. Not assisting low-achieving students when they are struggling (i.e., using less prompts to elicit responses, asking fewer follow-up questions)
6. Criticizing low-expectation students more often than high-achieving students for class participation
7. Praising low-expectation students less often than high-expectation students after positive class participation
8. Praising low-expectation students more regularly than high-expectation students for marginal or inadequate public responses
9. Providing low achievers with less accurate and less detailed feedback than that given to high achievers
10. Failing to provide low-achieving students with feedback about their responses as often as high-expectation students
11. Requiring less work and effort from low-achievers than from high-achieving students
12. Interrupting the performance of low-achievers more frequently than high achievers.

The concept of requiring high expectations for all students does not suggest that we should provide identical treatment for all students. The authors believe "that having high expectations and low tolerance for inappropriate behavior" should be expected for all students. According to Jones et al. (2016) in classrooms for student with E/BD, it is critical not to allow our frustrations with student's behavior to impact how we view and respond to the student's academic work.

We must consistently affirm high expectations for student academic and social behaviors and communicate these expectations by continuing to obtain the student's input during instructional activities and providing appropriate feedback regarding students' work and effort. One additional concept related to expectations regarding student behavior is the aspect of student behavior that teachers value most. The literature indicates that virtually all teachers place the highest value on four behaviors:

1. ability to control one's behavior during conflicts with peers
2. ability to control one's behavior during conflicts with teachers
3. following adult directions/requests
4. staying focused during instruction (Lane, Pierson, Stang, and Carter, 2010).

While it is necessary to assist students with E/BD to reduce behaviors that disrupt the classroom, it is equally important to ensure they develop the skills necessary for students to be successful in their classrooms and in their lives.

INDICATIONS OF GOOD RELATIONSHIPS WITH CHILDREN AND YOUTH

It is critical to evaluate if you have good relationships with your students in order to provide a therapeutic classroom environment in your class-room. The following are indications of having good relationships with students:

- Students follow your instructions
- Students help out and volunteer
- Students talk to you informally
- Students give you gifts
- Students reciprocate jokes and teasing
- Students give you compliments and praise you
- Students are in close proximity consistently (e.g., hang around be-fore going to lunch, they hang around before going home for the day),

If you can't tell if you have a strong relationship with your students, ask your colleagues to observe in your room, ask your colleagues to monitor your praise statements during an observation.

THE IMPORTANCE OF LISTENING SKILLS

William Glasser (1988) stated that students' attempts to be heard are the source of 95 percent of all aberrant behavior in schools. When we listen to students we provide them with a sense of significance as well as power (two key aspects of positive self-esteem). Being listened to makes individuals feel cared for and valued.

We need to ensure that there is ample time to hear the voices of students with E/BD. It may include frequent class meetings in which students are asked to share their joys, appreciations, and concerns regarding what is happening at school. In addition, paraphrasing is an effective way to let students recognize that you have listened to them and are trying to understand them. Johnson and Johnson (1975) listed seven general guidelines for effective paraphrasing:

1. Restate the sender's expressed ideas and feelings in our own words rather than mimic or echoing their exact words.
2. We proceed paraphrased remarks with, "You think . . . ,' "Your position is . . . ," "It seems to you that . . . ," "You feel that . . . ," and so on.
3. Avert any indications of approval or disapproval.
4. Make your nonverbal messages consistent with your verbal paraphrasing; look attentive, interested, and open to the sender's ideas and feelings, and demonstrate that you are concentrating on what the sender is trying to convey.
5. Express as accurately as possible what you heard the sender say and describe the feelings and attitudes involved.
6. Do not add to or subtract from the sender's message.
7. Put yourself in the sender's shoes and try to identify what it is they are feeling and what their message means.

SUMMARY

By having a good relationship with students, teachers can offer to students chances to be motivated and feel engaged in the learning process. Good teaching involves positive communication between the teacher and students. The best productivity in a classroom comes from effective cooperation between the teacher and the students. Strategies to develop positive teacher-student relations are one of the largest portions of your discipline plan. Some techniques that are easy to integrate into your everyday interactions with students include active listening skills, communicating positive expectations, correcting students in a constructive way, developing positive classroom pride, demonstrating caring, and preventing and reducing your own frustration and stress.

TEN TIPS FOR TEACHERS

1. Greet your students at the door at the beginning of the day.
2. Get to know your students' interests and likes.
3. Attend a student's community activities (e.g., sporting event, play, dance recital).
4. Make positive phone calls home at least on a weekly basis.
5. Be respectful to students at all times.
6. Talk to students about yourself (e.g., where you grew up, your hobbies).
7. Maintain a high rate of positive to negative statements.
8. Communicate caring and support toward all students.
9. Communicate high expectations to all students.
10. Give students eye contact when giving them corrective feedback.

QUESTIONS FOR DISCUSSION

1. Name some positive outcomes for developing positive relationships with your students.
2. How will you increase your use of positive versus negative statements when talking to your students?
3. Name steps a teacher can take to avoid negative interactions with low achieving students.
4. What are some of the steps a teacher can take to evaluate the strength of the relationship they have with their students?
5. Once you have evaluated your relationship with your students, what steps can be taken to improve those relationships?

REFERENCES

Allday, A., Hinkson-Lee, K., Hudson, T., Neilsen-Gatti, S., Kleinke, A., and Russel, C. (2012). Training general educators to increase behavior-specific praise: Effects on students with EBD. *Behavioral Disorders, 37,* 87–98.

Austin, J., and Soeda, J. (2008). Fixed-time teacher attention to decrease off-task behaviors of typically developing third graders. *Journal of Applied Behavior Analysis, 41,* 279–83.

Birch, S. H. and Ladd, G. W. (1997). The teacher-child relationship and children's early school adjustment. *Journal of School Psychology, 35,* 61–79.

Birnamen, C., and Page, F. (2012). Reflective practice creates a therapeutic preschool: Using relationships to heal trauma: 1. *Young Children, 67,* 40–48.

Bondy, E., Ross, D., Gallingane, C., and Hambacher, E. (2017). Creating environments of success and reliance: Culturally responsive classroom management and more. *Urban Education, 42,* 326–28.

Burchinal, M. R., Peisner-Feinberg, E., Pianta, R., and Howes, C. (2002). Development of academic skills from preschool through second grade: Family and classroom predictors of developmental trajectories. *Journal of School Psychology, 40,* 415–36.

Cancio, E. J., and Johnson, J. W. (2013). Designing effective class-wide motivation systems for students with Emotional and Behavioral Disorders. *Preventing School Failure: Alternative Education for Children and Youth, 57(1),* 49–57.

Catalano, R., Haggerty, K., Oesterle, S., Fleming, C., and Hawkins, J. (2004). The importance of bonding to school for healthy development: Findings from the social development research group. *Journal of School Health, 74,* 252–61.

Center on the Developing Child at Harvard University (2015). *Supportive relationships and active skill-building strengthen the foundations of resilience* (Working paper no. 13). Cambridge, MA: Author.

Cheney, D., Stage, S., Hawken, L., Lynass, Mielenz, C., and Waugh, M. (2009). A two-year outcome study of the check, connect, and expect intervention for students at-risk of severe behavior problems. *Journal of Emotional and Behavioral Disorders, 17,* 225–43.

Cook, B., Tankersley, M., Cook, L., and Landrum, T. (2000). Teachers' attitudes toward their included students with disabilities. *Exceptional Children, 67,* 115–35.

Cooper, H., and Good, T. (1983). *Pygmalion grows up.* New York: Longman.

Corbett, D., and Wilson, B. (2002). What urban students say about good? *Educational Leadership, 60,* 18–22.

Crone, D., Hawken, L., and Horner, R. (2010). *Responding to problem behavior in schools: The behavior education program* (2nd Ed.). New York: Guilford.

Dods, J. (2013). Enhancing understanding of the nature and supportive school-based relationship for youth who have experienced trauma. *Canadian Journal of Education, 36,* 71–95.

Dunn, A. (2010). We know you are Black at heart, A self-study of a white, suburban, urban high school teacher. In A. J. Stairs and Donnell (Eds.), *Research on urban teacher learning: Examining conceptual factors over tine* (pp. 29–40). Charlotte, NC: Information Age.

Glasser, W. (1988). On students' needs and team learning: A conversation with William Glasser. R. Brandt (Ed.). *Educational Leadership, 45,* 38–45.

Gregory, A., and Ripski, M. (2008). Adolescent trust in teachers: Implications for behaviors in high school classrooms. *The School Psychology Review, 37,* 337–53.

Gunter, P., Jack, S., and Depaepe, P. (1994). Effects of challenging behaviors of students with EBD on teacher instructional behavior. *Preventing School Failure, 38,* 35–39.

Hamre, B. K., and Pianta, R. C. (2001). Early-teacher-child relationships and the trajectory of children's school outcomes through eighth grade. *Child Development, 72(2),* 625–38.

Hugues, J. N. Luo, W., Kwok, O., and Loyd, L. (2008). Teacher-student support, effort full engagement, and achievement: A three-year longitudinal study. *Journal of Educational psychology, 100,* 1–14.

Johnson, D., and Johnson, R. (1975). *Learning togther and alone: Group theory and group skills.* Englewood Cliffs, NJ: Prentice Hall.

Jones, M., Bailey, R., Brion-Meiesels, G., and Partee, A. (2016). Choosing to be positive. *Educational Leadership, 74(1)* 63–68.

Jones, V., Greenwood, A., and Dunn, C. (2016). *Effective supports for students with emotional and behavioral disorders: A continuum of services.* Boston, MA: Pearson.

Jones, V., Dohrn, E., and Dunn, C. (2004). *Creating effective programs for students with emotional and behavior disorders: Interdisciplinary approaches for adding meaning and Hope to behavior change interventions.* Boston, MA: Pearson.

Kauffman, J. (1997). *Characteristics of emotional and behavior disorders of children and youth* (6th Ed.). Upper Saddle River, NJ: Merrill.

Ladd, G. W., Birch, S. H., and Buhs, E. S. (1999). Children's social and scholastic lives in kindergarten: Related spheres of influence? *Child Development, 70(6),* 1373–400.

Lane, K., Pierson, M., Stang, K., and Carter, E. (2010). Teacher expectations for student's classroom behavior: Do expectations vary as a function of school risk. *Remedial and Special Education, 31,* 163–74.

Marzano, R., Marzano, J., and Pickering, D. (2003). *Classroom management that works.* Alexandria, VA: Association for Supervision and Curriculum Development.

Meehan, B. T., Hughes, J. N., and Cavell, T. A. (2003). Teacher-student relationships as compensatory resources for aggressive children. *Child Development, 74,* 1145–57.

Mihalas, S., Morse, W., Allsop, D., and McHattan, P. (2009). Cultivating caring relationships between teachers and secondary students with emotional and behavioral disorders. *Remedial and Special Education, 30,* 108–25.

Musti-Rao, S., and Haydon, T. (2011). Strategies to increase behavior specific praise in an inclusive environment. *Intervention in School and Clinic, 47,* 91–97.

Nelson, J., Maculan, A., Roberts, M., and Ohlund, B. (2011). Sources of occupational stress for teachers of students with emotional and behavioral disorders. *Journal of Emotional and Behavioral Disorders, 9,* 123–30.

Noguera, P. (1995). Preventing and producing violence: A critical analysis of responses to school violence. *Harvard Education Review, 65,* 189–212.

O'Leary, D., and O'Leary, S. (1977). *Classroom management: The successful use of behavior modification* (2nd Ed.) New York: Pergamon Press.

Pianta, R., and Stuhlman, M. (2004). Teacher-child relationships and child success in the first year in school. *School Psychology Review, 33,* 444–58.

Riley, J., Mckevitt, B., Shriver, M., and Allen, K. (2011). Increasing on-task behavior using teacher attention delivered in a fixed-time schedule. *Journal of Behavioral Education, 20,* 149–62.

Rimm-Kaufman, S. E., and Hamre, K. K. (2010). The role of psychological science and efforts to improve teacher quality. *Teachers College Record, 112,* 2988–3023.

Scott, T., Alter, P., and Hirn (2011). An examination of typical classroom context and instruction for students with and without behavioral disorders. *Education and Treatment of Children, 34,* 619–41.

Shores, R., Gunther, P., and Jack, S. (1993). Classroom management strategies: Are they setting events for coercion, *Behavioral Disorders, 18,* 92–102.

Shores, R., and Wehby, J. (1999). Analyzing the classroom social behavior of students with EBD. *Journal of Emotional and Behavioral Disorders, 7,* 194–99.

Simpson, R., Peterson, R., and Smith, C. (2011). Critical educational program components for students with emotional and behavioral disorders: Science policy and practice. *Remedial and Special Education, 32,* 230–42.

Sutherland, K., Wehby, J., and Copeland, S. (2000). Effects of varying rates of behavior-specific praise on the on-task behavior of students with EBD. *Journal of Emotional and Behavioral Disorders, 8,* 2–8.

Tsai, S., and Cheney, D. (2012). The impact of adult-child relationship on school adjustment for children at risk of serious behavior problems. *Journal of Emotional and Behavioral Disorders, 20,* 105–14.

Van Acker, R., Grant, S., and Henry, D. (1996). Teacher and student behavior as a function of risk for aggression. *Education and Treatment of Children, 19,* 316–34.

Wilner, K. A., Kirigin, K. A., Braukmann, C. J., and Wolf, M. M. (1997). The training and validation of youth-preferred social behaviors of child-care personnel. *Journal of Applied Behavioral Analysis, 10*(2), 219–30.

Woolfolk, A., and Weinstein, C. (2006). Students and teachers' belief and perspectives about classroom management. In C. Evertson and C. Weinstein (Eds.), *Handbook of classroom management: Research, practice, and contemporary issues.* Mahwah, NJ: Lawrence Erlbaum.

Wright, T. (2013). "I keep me safe": Risk and resilience in children with messy lives. *Kappan, 95,* 39–43.

5

WE CAN'T DO IT ALONE—THE IMPORTANCE OF COLLABORATION

Mrs. Wellington has been working with students with significant emotional/behavioral disorders in a self-contained classroom for over ten years. She works well with her students and many parents are appreciative of the progress she makes with their children. While they appreciate the written communication that she provides through the home-school journals, some parents have gotten upset about the negative comments she writes in those journals.

Evaluations of her that are based on observations are very positive; however, there are complaints from other teachers and colleagues who work with her students. They complain that she doesn't want to work with them. When they ask her for help, she says she doesn't have time to help them.

When bus drivers have asked her to work with them to establish a behavior management plan for bus behavior, she tells them that is not her responsibility. When the teachers receive her students in general education classes, she never seems to have time to work with them to brainstorm solutions to problems they are facing. The speech/language therapists and the occupational therapists report that she doesn't keep them up to date on student progress.

STANDARDS

Council for Exceptional Children Initial Preparation Standard 7.0:
Collaboration. Beginning special education professionals collaborate with families, other educators, related service providers, individuals with exceptionalities across a range of learning experiences.

CHAPTER OBJECTIVES

Readers will be able:

1. To articulate the role of collaboration in working together with all
   the educational partners who work with our students.
2. To list the skills necessary to collaborate effectively.
3. To articulate the role of the educator in working together with other
   individuals who share our vision of helping students with emotion-
   al/behavioral disorders.

KEY VOCABULARY TERMS

Collaboration—The process of working together for a shared positive
purpose, focusing on the needs of the student. The process involves
all participants recognizing that they have an equal role in the
process and one person's work is not superior to another's.

Active Listening—The process of listening to understand the meaning
of what is being said, rather than to respond.

Co-Teaching—A method of delivering instruction in which two or
more educators deliver instruction in the general education class to
a diverse group of students (Cook and Friend, 1995).

Wraparound Services—The process of bringing together various community agencies and other supports with the family to provide
needed supports to assist the student.

Compassion—Involves the ability to "understand and care about what
another person feels, but do not attempt to feel it ourselves" (Tomlinson and Murphy, 2018, p. 23).

In working with students with emotional/behavioral challenges, we have to work together with many individuals and agencies. Juvenile Justice and child welfare agencies serve a significant number of our students who exhibit emotional/behavioral disorders (Malmgren and Meisel, 2002). Our students are often involved with multiple agencies, attend special education and general education classes, and have related services, paraprofessionals assigned to them, special transportation, and parents who are stressed as they struggle to cope with the many challenges of raising their child. We have to collaborate with these groups to ensure that our students are accepted within the school community among individuals who may have a low level tolerance for their behavior.

SKILLS NEEDED TO COLLABORATE

When teachers are able to work together to plan and implement interventions, there is a strong effect size on student achievement (Hattie, 2008). When families receive support from teachers and other educational professionals, there is evidence that they are more likely to implement effective strategies at home (McCleskey et al., 2017).

Collaboration is often defined as "working together." To work together requires several components that we need to analyze. Collaboration is different than consultation. In consultation, there is an assumption that the "consultant" has more expertise than the other members of a team. In collaboration, all members are equal partners coming to the table with shared expertise.

Appreciation of Others' Efforts

Each time an individual does any act, no matter how small, we need to recognize it. The motto for working with students with behavior problems is: "Never take good behavior for granted." That same motto should apply in our work with all our colleagues. We need to be grateful and thank everyone with whom we work for what they did that we appreciated. Griffith (2018) calls this "practicing gratitude" (Griffith, 2018, p. 64). There are actually apps and websites that provide gratitude practices.

Being grateful for what others do and communicating that gratitude to the individual makes that person feel appreciated and also builds a positive attitude within the person who appreciated the other's efforts. Recognizing any positive act through verbal comments, through gratitude notes, and other means builds a positive rapport that is necessary to be an effective collaborator.

When we build a system of positive communication, people look forward to being around us and gratitude becomes contagious and yields a positive climate.

When we model gratitude, students also follow. Happiness leads to success and higher achievement (Cunningham and Rainville, 2018). We are a role model for those around us.

Respecting Roles

When we collaborate, we recognize the roles of our partners in the process. We value what they have to say and what they do. We work to understand what their position entails. Think about you as a special educator believing that you are the expert in working with children with behavioral problems. You believe you know more than the general education teacher, yet that teacher may have taught longer than you or may have specific talents in working with students with behavior challenges that you don't have. Because of that individual's role, they may bring a different perspective.

Included in respecting roles is the necessity of putting aside our biases. Before we can do that, we need to recognize that we may be biased against certain individuals because of what they represent to us. Mrs. Wellington had a bad encounter with a social worker about five years ago; after that experience she has been very negative to social workers. She has developed a bias against them even though now she is working with a highly competent one. She is having a difficult time putting that bias and those feelings aside, but she needs to do that in order to respect the role of the individual.

In another instance, which happens more frequently than we would like to think, Mrs. Wellington had a negative experience with a case worker at the child welfare agency. As a result, she doesn't want to work cooperatively with that agency. However, it is critical that she set aside her bias and respect the role of the child welfare caseworkers in meeting the needs of her students.

Educators may have harmful preconceptions for some parents, because they live in poverty or don't have higher goals for their children. However, when school personnel engage parents in dialogue as equals, they will see that the parents do have goals for their children (Barnwell, 2018).

Trust

The Individual's ability to trust is influenced by whether they believe that others are acting appropriately in their own roles (Berg, Connolly, Lee, and Fairley, 2018). A first step in building that trust is for the educator to explain what their role is and how they see their role in helping the student. Trust promotes engagement. If people trust each other, they become more actively involved in the group dynamic. As a result, there is increased productivity (Berg, Connolly, Lee, and Fairley, 2018). When we trust others, we are excited to complete our tasks because we see our work as a partnership rather than feeling like we are isolated. People want to rely on us and if we do our part in a responsibility we can gain their trust.

Acceptance

Acceptance involves the ability to take the person the way they are and where they are, rather than trying to change them or making unrealistic demands on them. We may be working with a parent who has been abusive to their child but is in treatment to change his behavior. We may not believe that they will change but we still have to accept them and the fact that they are who they are and our role is to work cooperatively with them to meet the needs of the child.

Active Listening

One of the critical components of active listening is to truly listen to understand rather than listening to reply. Often when we are talking to others, it is almost as if we are waiting for a void in the conversation so we can reply, rather than adopting an attitude that we are listening to better understand how the individual perceives a situation.

An integral part of this process is listening to clarify and giving feed-back to the parent or another teacher based on what they have said. As an example, the parent may say the following and a responsible reply to clarify meaning can be the following:

> **Parent Statement:** I can't understand why you can't make Jamaray behave. You're doing something wrong. Jamaray has no problems at home, only at school!
>
> **Educator Response:** It sounds like you're saying that you're concerned about Jamaray's behavior in my class. Sounds like Jamaray is doing well at home. What kinds of things does he do well at home?

In active listening, we don't become defensive, we work to gather more information and stress that we want to work together for the benefit of the child. This is easier said than done particularly when the parent or another teacher or an administrator is attacking us. Arguing with the parent is non-productive and does not establish us as a role model of peaceful behavior.

Compassion

Compassion involves the ability to "understand and care about what another person feels, but do not attempt to feel it ourselves" (Tomlinson and Murphy, 2018, p. 23). We have to be able to understand what someone is going through from their viewpoint and we have to understand their needs. In many cases, their needs may be very different than ours are, but we have to be open-minded.

Picture this scenario, Mrs. Cobden is a teacher of students with emotional/behavioral disorders and she believes that one of her students needs more services from the speech/language pathologist. She becomes upset that the speech/language pathologist doesn't agree with her. Mrs. Cobden is upset and is speaking negatively about the speech/language pathologist in the teachers' lounge.

Mrs. Cobden should have discussed this situation with the speech/language pathologist. She would have then learned that the SLP is working long hours because the district has given her ten more students since the beginning of the school year and she is frustrated and doesn't see that she can give more services. She feels she is stretched as far as she can be.

This is an important skill also to remember when we are working with parents. We expect them to do two to three hours of homework with their child after they have worked all day and come home and cooked dinner for their four children. If we have compassion, we understand that parent's situation and recognize that we may be making unrealistic demands on that parent who is exhausted.

Positive Communication

There is a reason that many parents of students with emotional/behavioral disorders don't publicize their phone number and don't give it to school personnel. They only received phone calls when their child was in trouble. They dreaded the call from school because they knew it was bad news.

By the time their children get to secondary school, the parents are overwhelmed with the negative feedback received from the school and divorce themselves from school personnel because they are tired of being bombarded with negative news. Data has shown us that parent engagement decreases significantly after elementary and middle school with the exception of contact with a guidance counselor because parents are concerned about post-secondary plans (Barnwell, 2018).

How can we turn the tide and provide positive communication with parents, communicating a sense of camaraderie and collaboration We should monitor our behavior to determine whether we are giving parents positive feedback on a frequent basis. When a parent sends the child to school every day, we need to thank them. When a parent helps a child with homework, we need to thank them. A brief note means a lot to a parent.

Shared Responsibility

As we acquire these collaborative skills, we then have to put them in place as we work in a variety of collaborative roles. Shared responsibility builds trust because we trust people who follow through and complete tasks they say they will do. If we say we will send some resources home with the child and we don't do it, we destroy trust because we are sending the message that we don't follow up with what we say we will do.

As part of that responsibility, we have to reach out to others. We can't wait for them to contact us. We have to take the first step. We may complain that we haven't heard from someone like the school psychologist or the occupational therapist, and we don't know what they are doing with a student. If that is the case, we need to contact them rather than waiting and hoping to hear.

In collaboration we all work together to achieve a goal and we all have a responsibility to do what we are supposed to do as part of the team. We want to communicate with our fellow team members that when we accept a responsibility, we follow through and complete that responsibility.

COLLABORATION WITH OTHER AGENCIES

The complex, multiple, and intensive needs of our students with emotional/behavioral challenges result in the critical need for us to collaborate with other agencies (Malmgren and Meisel, 2002). Our students may be involved in agencies such as mental health child care, substance abuse, truant officers, juvenile justice, and other systems of support. As educators we must work with the liaisons from these agencies that are assigned to each of our students.

Our role is twofold: working with the agencies that are already involved in providing some type of service to the student and working with families to connect them to needed services. Parents may come to us in tears because they don't know how to control the behavior of their child, they suspect that their child is using drugs, or the child has attempted suicide. We should know what services are available in the community and how the parent can access those services. Our school social worker and school administrator are able to assist us in learning more about the services available.

One such approach available in some communities is the wraparound process. Wraparound is a collaborative process that brings together the families and the key agencies that are involved with the student to brainstorm the students' needs and matching services. They wrap the needed services as identified by the family around the student and the family. In wraparound, family members are empowered to be the essential contributors who identify needed solutions to the challenges they are facing. Informal supports such as churches, friends, and others may join the wraparound team. The supports that the family receives are from the community so they are easily accessible for the family (Quinn and Lee, 2007).

COLLABORATION WITH OTHER TEACHERS AND CO-TEACHING

We work as collaborators when we work together with other teachers in our buildings. We may be asked for behavior management advice, we may give each other ideas and materials, we may rely on other teachers to give us an idea about how other students at a particular grade level are doing and what the behavior of their students is.

We also work together with other teachers if we are teachers in instructional classes for students with special needs when we want to place our children back in general education classes. When we are doing this, we must proceed with caution and consider the needs and the schedule of the classroom teacher. We also have to have an open discussion about what the teacher expects from the students so we can teach our students what will be expected in a new setting.

If we are including one of our students in the classroom and sending a paraprofessional with the student, we need to collaborate with the classroom teacher and the paraprofessional so the paraprofessional understands both of our sets of expectations. It has been found that general education placements rates for students with emotional disturbance more than doubled between 1990 and 2007 (McLeskey, Landers, Williamson, and Hoppey, 2012). As a result, we must work closely with general education teachers.

Co-teaching is a common practice within schools today. In this process, the classroom teacher and the special education teacher share space within the general education classroom and work together to meet the needs of the students, including those students with disabilities. There are multiple models of co-teaching, such as one lead and one support, station teaching, alternative teaching, parallel teaching, and team teaching (McDuffie, Landrum, and Gelman, 2008).

Co-teaching has been described like a marriage of two individuals. Effective co-teaching is necessary to enjoin all the collaborative skills we talked about earlier in this chapter. The special education teacher is not an aide, they are in the classroom to work with students. When special educators work together in this role with general education teachers, it is critical that they establish a collaborative behavior management plan for the class. Both parties have to agree on what the expectations are for students, and what recognition students receive for following the rules, and what consequences are received when rules are not followed. Both educators need to also decide how they will teach the appropriate social skills.

It should be seen as an arrangement where evidence-based behavior management and instructional practices are delivered (McDuffie, Landrum, and Gelman, 2008). Co-teaching arrangements that have smaller student-teacher ratios have resulted in increased student engagement and academic achievement (Eschete, Mooney, and Lastrapes, 2016). When preparing for a co-teaching arrangement it is critical that there be adequate co-planning time, respect for each other, administrative support, and frequent reflection and evaluation of the process (Friend and Cook, 2013; Jackson et al., 2017).

Student outcomes related to co-teaching suggest that educators should be very careful when implementing co-teaching and should plan well in advance of its implementation (Jackson et al., 2017). Conderman and Hedin (2015) stress the importance of differentiation within the co-taught classroom and that differentiation should include choices for students, flexible grouping systems, presentation of content at various skill levels, utilizing different assessments and products, attention to student affect, meaningful activities and processes, and the creation of a respectful learning environment.

COLLABORATION WITH OTHER INDIVIDUALS WITHIN THE SCHOOL WHO ARE WORKING WITH THE STUDENTS—PARAPROFESSIONALS, BUS DRIVERS, CAFETERIA WORKERS, RELATED SERVICES PROFESSIONALS

The role of teachers has expanded as schools are hiring more paraprofessionals (Giangreco, Suter, and Hurley, 2011). Teachers who entered the field expecting to work with students in today's schools, are now supervisors of other adults. Paraprofessionals play an integral role in working with students with disabilities but are supervised by the teachers.

The clear establishment of roles and responsibilities should be done before the school year starts. Teachers must sit down with paraprofessionals and let them know exactly what their role expectations are. Paraprofessionals support instruction planned by teachers; they don't plan instruction. Paraprofessionals are not responsible for the direct education of students; that responsibility rests with the teacher.

The skills that have been established earlier in this chapter apply to working with paraprofessionals. The teacher must understand and communicate the role of the paraprofessionals and respect that role. When the lines of who is responsible for what get blurred, the educator needs to talk openly as soon as possible with the paraprofessional. The educator needs to engage in active listening and needs to clarify responsibilities. The educator also serves as a role model, providing examples of positive behavior management.

The teacher needs to provide training to the paraprofessional and should also be involved in the training of bus drivers and cafeteria workers. While the teacher may be busy working with students, he must also communicate with other staff members what his positive behavior management system entails. Teachers have to educate others about what type of program they are utilizing and should enlist the support of the paraprofessionals, bus drivers, and cafeteria workers.

These support staff want assistance, so we should provide it. We may complain that they are too negative about the student. When we hear such a complaint we have to ask ourselves if we have modeled appropriate behavior and shared with the individuals what we are utilizing.

It is important to establish positive systems for bus drivers, which provides support to the drivers and also establishes the bus and the classroom as important settings for the students. As an example, for the bus, there could be a positive bus system like white slips used as a reward for desired behaviors. In this situation, if the student has done well on the bus to school and the bus home, the driver can give the students a white slip for each appropriate behavior (Johns, 2018). At the end of each trip, the driver gives the students a white slip, which the student then brings in the classroom. The teacher puts all the white slips in a jar and has a drawing at the end of the day for a prize that the teacher has chosen or a choice of prizes. A similar system can be established in the cafeteria.

Some teachers are reluctant to provide too much information to the bus driver, paraprofessional, or cafeteria worker, fearing that they will violate confidentiality laws. It is important to remember that information should be shared with an individual when they have a right to know the information in order to do their job (Johns, 2016). For example, it would be important for a teacher to share information that the student has a seizure disorder with the bus driver. It would be important to share information about children's allergies with the cafeteria. At the same time, there is a necessity to train these individuals on confidentiality laws.

Support Services Personnel

Students with emotional/behavioral challenges are involved with related services personnel within the school. They may be receiving speech/ language services, they are seeing the school social worker, the school psychologist may be collecting assessment data about them, the school nurse may be seeing them because of health problems, the occupational or physical therapist may be seeing them because of sensory issues or large or small motor problems. Our collaboration with these individuals is critical. We are part of a team that is helping the student. If we are not receiving regular reports, we need to reach out to receive those. We also need to communicate that we are willing to follow up with whatever skills they are working on.

Picture this, the social worker comes into your classroom to work with your students on social skills. You are delighted because you see this as an opportune time to take a break. The social worker perceives that you don't think what she is doing is important because you don't observe and you can't do any follow up. It is very important to support what the social worker is doing by observing and by reinforcing the skills throughout the week in the classroom.

COLLABORATION WITH ADMINISTRATORS

One of the most frequent reasons that special education teachers cite for leaving the field is lack of administrative support (Albrecht, Johns, Mountsteven, and Olufunmilola, 2009; Cancio, Albrecht, and Johns, 2013). Administrators often perceive that they don't have the expertise in special education and therefore leave teachers alone. Teachers then perceive that they are being ignored and devalued.

Before teachers can make that assumption, they need to reach out to their administrators, keeping them informed about what they are doing, inviting them to visit their class, and asking for their advice when dealing with a difficult situation. Some teachers are guilty of leaving the school administrator out of the loop because they are used to making their own decisions. Administrators are not happy when they learn that the teacher has done something, like soliciting funds outside of school or sending a student home, without telling them.

In order to build trust between the teacher and the administrator, communication is a must and soliciting assistance is critical rather than acting unilaterally.

COLLABORATION WITH FAMILIES

We have to work even harder to establish positive relationships with families of students with emotional/behavioral challenges because many of the parents have only heard from the school when there was a problem. They are reluctant to even come to school or answer a phone call because they are worn out from hearing the negative messages. We have to turn that around and establish positive relationships with the parents and build trust.

Many years ago, we did home visits but then there was a movement against those for a number of reasons, including safety. Home visits are now coming back with the provision that teachers don't go into homes alone. Social workers or psychologists, administrators, or counselors may accompany the teacher.

When planning a home visit, be very cautious about whether the parent may not want educators in their home because they are embarrassed by their living arrangements. If that is the case and they are uncomfortable about coming into the school because of previous negative experiences, consider meeting with them at a neutral site such as a coffee shop or a library.

If parents are comfortable with coming into school, make them feel welcome by making the environment a friendly one. When possible, offer coffee or cookies. Respect their time by being on time and planning an adequate time period to answer their questions. Provide examples of what the student can do.

Just as we reinforce our students for positive behavior, we need to reinforce parents for all they do. If they help their child with homework, thank them. If they get their children to school every day and on time, thank them. If they come for conferences, thank them. Remember the principle of an attitude of gratitude for everything that the parent does to support you.

Parents of children with emotional/behavioral disorders are struggling to meet the needs of the child and the entire family. They need our support when they are in crisis. We need to know what services are available for them and connect the family to needed help.

We can also provide information and resources for parents and seek feedback from them on how they want to work together—do they prefer an email or a phone call, do they prefer to come to school to meet or meet at another location, what kind of resource information they would like from us (Johns, Crowley, and Guetzloe, 2002).

There is a word of caution. We may find parents who want to call during the school day or want to call after school and talk for over an hour. It is critical to establish parameters for when we are available to talk. If the parent needs more assistance than we can provide, we will want to refer the parent to the social worker or counselor. The parent may have intense needs and therefore needs to be provided more assistance than we are able to provide.

Many teachers now utilize home-school journals as a way to communicate with parents. These can be very helpful to both parents and the teachers if they are done correctly. They can also become very negative and establish an adversarial relationship between the parent and the teacher. When we make statements about what the child has done that day, we need to carefully craft the information so that it is factual rather than opinion and it is helpful to the parent rather than being discouraging to them. While we may be the bearer of bad news, we can word that news in such a way that is non-judgmental and non-critical to the parent.

Let's look at some examples:

Instead of writing this . . .

Desiree had a bad day. She wouldn't pay attention.

... Write this:

Today, Desiree was able to stay on task for three minutes at a time. She was distracted by the weather outside and asked several questions during the day about it.

Instead of writing this ...

Bart can't get along with the other students.

... Write this:

We are working on getting Bart to keep his hands to himself. He wants to shove other students when he is in the hall and shoved five students today.

Instead of writing this ...

Jenny is not reading at the same level as the other third graders in clas.

... Write this:

Jenny is currently reading independently at a beginning second grade level and we are working on increasing her reading time in the classroom.

IN SUMMARY

As educators we can't work in isolation. We have to rely on others to be successful with our students. Students with emotional/behavioral disorders need all the services that are available, so a large part of our job is networking and reaching out to others who can help our students. Collaboration is an integral part of our role and we have to know what services are available, where they are available, and all of the people that can help us help our students.

TEACHING TIPS

1. Adopt an attitude of gratitude. Look for positive actions that others take and then thank the individuals for those actions. Recognize positive behavior in others.
2. Send frequent positive notes home to parents about what their child did well at school. Set a goal to send a specific number of positive notes home each week.
3. Follow through with what you were supposed to do for members of your team, because this makes you a responsible partner in the collaborative process.
4. Reach out to those with whom you are working rather than waiting for them to reach out to you. Shared responsibility means that you must communicate when others may not.
5. Educate yourself on the agencies and services that are available within your community so that you can refer families when they are seeking assistance.
6. Provide supportive assistance to other staff within your school to build rapport.
7. When planning any co-teaching arrangement, planning ahead and frequently are essential to success.
8. Work with bus drivers and cafeteria workers to establish positive behavior management systems within those settings.
9. Reinforce the work of related services personnel in your classroom.
10. When establishing parent conferences, make the environment welcoming and friendly and respect the needs of the parent. Be appreciative of all the efforts the parent makes.

QUESTIONS FOR DISCUSSION

1. Think about someone with whom you were working on a project and you had difficulty accomplishing the task. What were the barriers to working together? What could you have done differently to improve your collaboration with the person?
2. Think about a written communication you received that was offensive to you. Why was it offensive? How could the sender convey the message in a positive manner?

REFERENCES

Albrecht, S., Johns, B., Mountsteven, J., and Olufunmilola, O. (2009). Working conditions as risk or resiliency factors for teachers of students with emotional and behavioral disabilities. *Psychology in the Schools. 46(10),* 1006–22.

Barnwell, P. (2018). Engaging high school parents. *Association for Supervision and Curriculum Development: Education Update. 60(2),* 2–3, 6.

Berg, J., Connolly, C., Lee, A., and Fairley, E. (2018). A matter of trust. *Educational Leadership, 75(6),* 56–61.

Cancio, E., Albrecht, S., and Johns, B. (2013). Defining administrative support and its relationship to the attrition of teachers of students with emotional and behavioral disorders. *Education and Treatment of Children 36(4),* 71–94.

Conderman, G., and Hedin, L. (2015). Differentiating instruction in co-taught classrooms for students with emotional/behaviour difficulties. *Emotional and Behavioural Difficulties, 20(4),* 349–61.

Cook, L. and Friend, M. (1995). Co-teaching: guidelines for creating effective practices. *Focus on Exceptional Children, 28,* 1–16.

Cunningham, K., and Rainville, K. (2018). Joyful leadership in practice. *Educational Leadership, 75(6),* 62–67.

Eschete, C., Mooney, and Lastrapes, R. (2016). *Increasing teacher education candidate collaboration knowledge and skill through approximations of practice.* Manuscript submitted for publication.

Friend, M., and Cook, L. (2013). *Interactions: Collaboration skills for school professionals.* Seventh Edition. Upper Saddle River, NJ: Pearson Education.

Giangreco, M., Suter, J., and Hurley, S. (2011). Revisiting personnel utilized in inclusion-oriented schools. *Journal of Special Education, 47(2),* 121–32.

Griffith, O. (2018). Creating the grateful school in four phases. *Educational Leadership, 75(6),* 64–65.

Hattie, J. (2008). Visible *learning: A synthesis of over 800 meta-analyses relating to achievement.* New York: Routledge.

Jackson, K., Willis, K., Giles, L., Lastrapes, R., and Mooney, P. (2017). How to meaningfully incorporate co-teaching into programs for middle school students with emotional and behavioral disorders. *Beyond Behavior, 26(1),* 11–18.

Johns, B. (2018). Reduction *of school violence: Alternatives to Suspension.* Fifth edition. Palm Beach Gardens, Florida: LRP Publications.

Johns, B. (2016). *Your classroom guide to special education law.* Baltimore: Brookes Publishing.

Johns, B., Crowley, E., and Guetzloe, E. (2002). *Effective curriculum for students with emotional and behavioral disorders.* Denver: Love Publishing.

Malmgren, K., and Meisel, S. (2002). Characteristics and service trajectories of youth with serious emotional disturbance in multiple service systems. *Journal of Child and Family Studies, 11(2),* 217–29.

McCleskey, J., Landers, E., Williamson, P., and Hoppey, D. (2012). Are we moving toward educating students with disabilities in less restrictive settings? *The Journal of Special education, 46,* 131–40.

McCleskey, J. et al. (2017). *High-leverage practices in special education.* Arlington, VA: Council for Exceptional Children and the CEEDAR Center.

McDuffie, K., Landrum, T., and Gelman, J. (2008). Co-teaching and students with emotional and behavioral disorders. *Beyond Behavior,* Winter 2008, 11–16.

Quinn, K., and Lee, V. (2007). The wraparound approach for students with emotional and behavioral disorders: Opportunities for school psychologists. *Psychology in the Schools, 44(1),* 101–11.

Tomlinson, C., and Murphy, M. (2018). The empathetic school. *Educational Leadership, 75(6),* 20–27.

6

PROMOTING LONGEVITY AND TAKING
CARE OF ONESELF

Mrs. Powell, a middle-school teacher of students with emotional and behavior disorders (E/BD), emphasizes that her job is extremely challenging. Her biggest issue is lack of administrative support. She reports, "I don't think my principal understands students with EBD or the IEP process." She would like her administrator to understand when she asks for help, she needs it immediately, not in twenty minutes. She is also concerned that her students need supervision throughout the day, which results in her not having a prep or lunch hour. Mrs. Powell copes by exercising after work, having a personal life outside of school, and remaining current in her field. Mr. Brown, a teacher for students with E/BD at an alternative school, had similar experiences with administrators in the past. He says, "The current issue I face is the large number of students with significant behavior problems, especially when they exhibit challenging behavior simultaneously in the same setting." Mr. Brown copes by leaving work at school, having a personal life outside of school, and talking to colleagues about his day-to-day frustrations. Mrs. Powell and Mr. Brown are like thousands of teachers of students with challenging behaviors across the country who want to make a positive impact on children or youth with E/BD. Their positions, however, often lead to frustration, stress, or fatigue. Without healthy coping skills and a support system, teachers like Mrs. Powell and Mr. Brown often leave the field feeling unappreciated and burned out.

STANDARDS

CEC Initial Preparation Standard 6.3—Special education specialists model and promote respect for all individuals and facilitate ethical professional practice.

CEC Initial Preparation Standard 6.4—Special education specialists actively participate in professional development and professional learning communities to increase professional knowledge and expertise.

CEC Initial Preparation Standard 6.5—Special education specialists plan, present, and evaluate professional development focusing on effective and ethical practice at all organizational levels.

CHAPTER OBJECTIVES

Readers will be able:

1. To recognize the signs of stress and burnout.
2. To develop an adaptive frame of mind to avoid stress.
3. To gain strategies that enhances relationships with administrators.

KEY VOCABULARY TERMS

Attrition—The rates at which teachers leave the field.

Adaptive frame of mind—The optimistic and positive manner in which you perceive your teaching assignment.

Burnout—A collapse or breakdown, either physical or emotional, caused by extreme pressure or stress.

Stress—Pressure or strain from adverse conditions.

SPECIAL EDUCATION TEACHER ATTRITION

As reported by the U.S. Department of Education, roughly 8.4 percent of the nation's teachers left the field in the academic year of 2003–2004 (Westervelt, 2016; Dillion, 2007). While 30 percent of the departing teachers retired, more than half of these teachers indicated they left to pursue another career or because they were dissatisfied (Albrecht, Johns, Mounsteven, and Olorunda, 2009).

The problem with teacher retention goes far beyond aging out through retirement, as nearly one-third of all new teachers leave the field after just three years due to dissatisfaction, acceptance of better jobs (e.g., administrative positions), or career diversion (Dillion, 2007). Unfavorable working conditions and/or school climate are cited as reasons for attrition and difficulty filling open positions in high-needs schools (Berry, Rasberry, and Williams, 2007).

Over 6 million children and youth in the public schools across the United States receive special education services (Roach, 2009), placing the need for highly qualified special educators well into the hundreds of thousands (Hanson, 2011). Given special education's long history of significant shortages of teachers (Boe et al., 2013), it is not surprising that forty-eight states are currently experiencing such shortages (Sutcher, Darling-Hammond, and Carver-Thomas, 2016).

To make the problem worse, few prospective teachers are willing to pursue special education as a career, and of those who do, roughly 9 percent leave the field after the first year (Horrison-Collier, 2013) and roughly 30 percent leave after three years (Dillon, 2007). Hanawar (2006) indicates that national attrition rates of special education teachers can be as high as 13.5 percent. McLesky, Tyler, and Flippin (2004), indicate that nationally between 7 percent and 15 percent of special education teachers leave annually.

Research indicates that the job of the special educator is difficult, demanding, and more stressful than that of general education teachers (Nagle and Brown, 2003). Additionally, special educators face increasing caseloads, lack of clarity in their roles, lack of administrative support, excessive paperwork, large caseloads, feelings of isolation and loneliness, and minimal collaboration with colleagues (Albrecht et al., 2009; Cancio and Conderman, 2008; Futernick, 2007; Kaff, 2004; Katsiyannis, Zhang, and Conroy, 2003; Prather-Jones, 2011; Schlichte, Yssel, and Merbler, 2005).

When special educators are overwhelmed with the stressors they face, they leave the field (Albrecht et al., 2009). An important issue to address, therefore, is whether current special educators are dealing with the pressures that accompany their jobs in healthy or unhealthy ways.

The main problem is not retirement as one may conclude; it is that almost one-third of new special education teachers leave the profession after three years in the field (Dillion, 2007). Students with E/BD can present intensive needs, requiring the intervention and instruction of well-trained and qualified teachers to work with them in the classroom (Albrecht et al., 2009; Katsiaannis et al., 2003; Prater-Jones, 2011; U.S. Department of Education, 2000).

The symptoms of stress and burnout may have far-reaching effects which impact the special education teacher both professionally and personally. This exposure to stress causes certain observable behaviors in teachers.

What allows special education teachers to have professional longevity while others leave the field or transfer to a regular education position is a complex phenomenon. Appendix J summarizes the research findings on special education attrition and retention over the two decades. It shows a broad range of factors linked to special education teacher attrition and retention. Some of the most common factors associated with stress, burnout, and attrition are: administrative support, teacher roles, large caseloads, service delivery, and job satisfaction.

Sources of stress and consequences of burnout reported in the literature that are associated with E/BD teacher stress and burnout are: decreased feelings of accomplishments (Embich, 2001; Pullis, 1992; Stiver, 1980; Zabel and Zabel, 1982), feeling overwhelmed (Pullis, 1992; Sweeney and Townley, 1993), lowered professional commitment (Nelson et al., 2001), difficulties with personal or professional relationships (Maslach and Jackson, 1984; Pullis, 1992; Stiver, 1980; Sweeney et al., 1993; Wrobel, 1993), personal accomplishments, neglect of other responsibilities, disruption of sleep patterns (Fimian and Santoro, 1983; Pullis, 1992), physical complaints (e.g., headaches, exhaustion) (Fimian and Santoro, 1983; Sweeney and Townley, 1993; Wrobel, 1993), emotional exhaustion (George et al., 1995; Zabel and Zabel, 1982), dealing with students in an impersonal way, feeling guilty for not providing an effective education for students (Pullis, 1992; Sweeney et al., 1993), increased use of alcohol and other substances, increased absences (Maslach and Jackson, 1984; Stiver, 1980; Sweeney et al., 1993), poor attitudes regarding students (Retish, 1986; Stiver, 1980), overreactions to mild work pressures (Stiver, 1980), detachment and distancing from students (Fimian and Santoro, 1983; Stiver, 1980), disruption of personal and professional life (Stiver, 1980;. Zabel, Boomer, and King, 1984), a cynical and dehumanizing view of students (Stiver, 1980; Zabel and Zabel, 1982), lower morale and creativity, and a disorganized classroom (Stiver, 1980; Zabel et al., 1984). See Appendix K for positive and negative factors to stay in the field.

Administrative Support

Principal support of teachers has been cited as one of the most important factors both for general and special educators' retention (Darling-Hammond, 2003). Principal leadership is a critical aspect of creating settings that support teachers to meet the complex and diverse needs of their students (Correa and Wagner, 2011).

In 2007, the Council for Children with Behavioral Disorders (CCBD) conducted a survey of school personnel working with students with E/BD to determine the key factors that result in them staying or exiting the field. This survey revealed that a significant factor in determining whether teachers were likely to stay versus likely to leave was administrative support (Albrecht et al., 2009).

The findings of the CCBD survey are consistent with earlier reports that administrative support is one of the most frequently cited causes of attrition (Littrell, Billingsley, and Cross, 1994; Billingsley and Cross, 1992; Schlichte, Yssel, and Merbler, 2005).

The Study of Personnel Needs in Special Education (2000) found that supportive administrators and colleagues might offset the negative effects of a burdensome workload. In addition, the Texas Center for Educational Research (2006) found that special education teachers who rated their working conditions adversely did not reflect a strong school climate in either the administrative or instructional domain.

Gersten, Keating, Yovanoff, and Harniss (2001) studied 887 special educators within three large urban school districts on the issues that related to their intention to stay in the field. Support from principals and teachers at the building level was found to have a strong effect on teachers' working conditions. The actions of the building principal and the other teaching staff are critical in establishing a positive school culture.

SIGNS OF STRESS AND BURNOUT

Stiver (1980) conducted a study to identify possible symptoms associated with stress and burnout for teachers of students with E/BD. He found that these symptoms either decreased the teacher's adaptive behaviors or increased problematic behaviors in and outside the classroom environment. These symptoms included personal and professional behaviors. Appendix K identifies these symptoms and behaviors.

Since the early 1980's special educators have investigated the problem of stress, burnout, and attrition. However, there has been little impact on the field of special education, especially, for teachers of students with E/BD. School districts and administrators must develop a systematic process to retain qualified and motivated teachers of students with E/BD. Most of the research-based strategies conducted on stress, burnout, and attrition have been correlational, descriptive, or survey in nature (Billingsley, 2004; Albrecht et al., 2009; Cancio et al., 2013). Limited research has been conducted on strategies to alleviate stress, burnout, and attrition of special education teachers (Cancio and Conderman, 2007).

Factors and strategies that can influence the success of longevity for teachers of students with E/BD fall into six categories: (a) developing an adaptive frame of mind; (b) developing positive relationships with colleagues; (c) strategies for organization, time management, and upcoming activities; (d) change, innovation, and new opportunities; (e) self-assessment of stress and burnout; and (f) coexisting and developing relationships with administrators. The preceding six factors and strategies in promoting longevity will be discussed below (Cancio and Conderman, 2007).

DEVELOPING AN ADAPTIVE FRAME OF MIND

The manner in which you perceive your teaching assignment has a significant impact on job satisfaction. Consequently, attitudes toward your students, your teaching assignment, and yourself are essential elements in promoting longevity. The following are strategies to assist in developing an adaptive frame of mind:

Developing Positive Relationships with Colleagues

Due to the responsibilities and workload for teachers of students with E/BD, teachers tend to isolate themselves and rarely interact with colleagues (Billingsley, Bodkins, and Hendricks, 1993; George et al., 1995; Morvant, 1995). They tend to work all day and spend most of the day in their classroom working on required tasks or supervising students. As you can imagine, taking breaks minimizes stress and allows you to become more effective in the classroom.

More importantly, by not taking breaks it affects your ability to develop relationships with colleagues. If you develop relationships with your colleagues, work is more enjoyable, and colleagues are more cooperative, collaborative, and can serve as a support system for you.

Strategies for Organization, Time Management, and Upcoming Activities

As mentioned earlier, E/BD teacher overload can lead to stress, burnout, and attrition (Billingsley et al., 1993; Billingsley, et.al., 1995; Cross and Billingsley, 1994; Gersten, et al., 2001; Morvant et al., 1995; Singh and Billingsley, 1996; and Westling and Whitten, 1996). Excessive paperwork, large caseloads, meetings, lack of time for teaching, and other responsibilities (e.g., bus duty, lunch room duties) are contributors to decisions to leave the field.

Teachers who are effective are organized and have clear and realistic expectations of themselves (Burnette and Peter-Johnson, 2004). Teachers who have the ability to reduce their stress have: good organizational skills, can set priorities, manage their time wisely, and are realistic of what they can accomplish in a set time period. Setting priorities and scheduling tasks are necessary skills needed in managing time and tasks effectively.

Strategies for Change, Innovation, and New Opportunities

Teachers who are successful and have longevity develop as individuals and educators. They keep up with current trends in the field, implement research into practice, and they evaluate the effectiveness of the practices they utilize in the classroom.

Teachers of students with E/BD need to be able to identify sources of stress and have the ability to implement strategies to curtail stress and burnout. The more mentally and physically healthy a teacher of students with E/BD is, the more effective they will be in the classroom.

Coexisting and Developing Relationships with Administrators

In a study conducted by George et al. (1995), they found that if teachers of student with E/BD perceived administrative support as adequate or more than adequate there was a greater likelihood that they planned to remain in the field. In a Nelson et al. study (2001), respondents reported lower levels of stress when they had a strong relationship with their principals.

One of the most frequently cited factors of stress, burnout, and attrition of teachers of students with E/BD reported in the literature is lack of administrative support (Billingsley et al., 1995; Cross and Billingsley, 1994; George et al., 1995; Gersten et al., 2001; Nelson et al., 2001; Singh and Billingsley, 1994; Westling and Whitten, 1996). Therefore, it is critical to develop and maintain a strong relationship with your principal/special education administrator.

To retain highly qualified teachers of students with E/BD, teachers and school districts need to promote and practice strategies that will allow them to enhance their longevity in the field. Hopefully increasing longevity of teachers can enhance the outcome measures for students with E/BD. See Appendix L for categories and strategies for reducing stress, and Appendix M for a checklist of strategies teachers can use to manage their stress in their environments.

TIPS FOR TEACHERS

1. Stay active after the work day (e.g., go to the gym, take walks, take a yoga class).
2. Evaluate if you have the symptoms of stress and burnout.
3. Improve your organizational skills.
4. Live a healthy lifestyle by eating well and getting enough sleep.
5. Maintain hope.
6. Form colleague relationships with others in your school.
7. Remain current in the field.
8. Communicate that it is all about the students.
9. Connect with E/BD teachers outside your school.

QUESTIONS FOR DISCUSSION

1. Think about a situation in which you were stressed. How did you cope positively or negatively with the situation?
2. How can teachers improve their working relationships with their administrators?
3. What are the ways in which an educator can take the time to get the physical exercise he or she needs?

REFERENCES

Albrecht, S., Johns, B., Mountsteven, J., Olorunda, O. (2009). Working conditions as risk or resiliency factors for teachers of students with emotional and behavioral disabilities. *Psychology in the Schools, 46(10),* 1006–22.

Boe, E. E., de Bettencourt, L. U., Dewey, J., Rosenberg, M., Sindelar, P., and Leko, C. (2013). Variability in demand for special education teachers: Indicators, explanations, and impacts. *Exceptionality, 21,* 103–25.

Berry, B., Rasberry, M., and Williams, A. (2007). Recruiting and retaining quality teachers for high needs schools: *Insights from NBCT summits and other policy initiatives. Hillsborough, NC: Center for Teaching Quality.* Retrieved April 5, 2008, from http://www.teaching quality.org/legacy/Nat_Strtegy_Forum.pdf.

Billingsley, B. S. (2004). Special education retention and attrition: A critical analysis of the research literature. *Journal of Special Education, 38(1),* 39–55.

Billingsley, B. S., Bodkins, D., and Hendricks, M. B. (1993). Why special educators leave teaching: implications for administrators. *Case in Point, 7(2),* 123–38.

Billingsley, B. S., Carlson, E., and Klein, S. (2004). The working conditions and induction support of early career special educators. *Exceptional Children, 70(3),* 333–47.

Billingsley, B.S., and Cross, L. (1992). Teacher's decisions to transfer from special to general education. *The Journal of Special Education, 24,* 496–511.

Billingsley, B.S., Pyecha, J., Smith-Davis, J., Murray, K., and Hendricks, M. (1995). *Improving retention of special education teachers: Final report.* (Prepared for the Office of Special Education Programs, Office of Special Education and Rehabilitative Services, U. S. Department of Education, Under Cooperative Agreement HO23!10001). ERIC Reproduction Service NO. ED379860.

Brownell, M. T., Smith, S. W., McNellis, J., and Miller, M. D. E. (1997). Attrition in special education: Why teachers leave the classroom and where they go. *Exceptionality, 7(3),* 143–55.

Burnette, J., and Peters-Johnson, C. (2004). *Thriving as a special educator: Balancing your practices and ideals.* Reston: VA, Council for Exceptional Children.

Cancio, E. J., Albrecht, S. F., and Johns, B. H. (2013). Defining administrative support and its relationship to the attrition of teachers of students with emotional and behavioral disorders. *Education and Treatment of Children, 36(4),* 71–94.

Cancio, E. J., and Conderman, G. (2008). Promoting longevity: Strategies for teachers of students with emotional and behavioral disorders. *Beyond Behavior, 17(3),* 30–36.

Correa, V. I., and Wagner, J. Y. (2011). Principals' role in supporting the induction of special education teachers. *Journal of Special Education Leadership, 24(1),* 17–25.

Cross, L. and Billingsley, B. S. (1994). Testing a model of special educators' intent to stay in teaching. *Exceptional Children, 60(5),* 411–21.

Darling-Hammond, L. (2003). Keeping good teachers: Why it matters, what leaders can do. *Educational Leadership, 60(8),* 6–13.

Dillion, S. (2007). With turnover high, schools fight for teachers. *The New York Times.* Retrieved August 27, 2007, from http://www.nytimes.com/2007/08/07/education/27teacher.html.

Embich, J. L. (2001). The relationship of secondary special education teachers' roles and factors that lead to professional burnout. *Teacher education and special education, 24(1),* 58–69.

Fimian, M. J., and Santoro, T. M. (1983). Sources and manifestations of occupational stress as reported by full-time special education teachers. *Exceptional Children, 46,* 540–43.

Futernick, K. (2007). *A possible dream: Retaining California teachers so all students learn.* Sacramento: The Center for Teacher Quality, California State University.

Gersten, R., Keating, T., Yovanoff, P., and Harniss, M. (2001). Working in special education: Factors that enhance special educators' intent to stay. *Exceptional Children, 67(4),* 549–71.

George, N. L., George, M. P., Gersten, R., and Grosenick, J. R. (1995). To leave or to stay: An exploratory study of teachers of students with emotional and behavioral disorders. *Remedial and Special Education, 16,* 227–36.

Hanawar, V. (2006). Alternative routes for special education teachers relieving shortages worsened by NCLB. *Education Week, 25(34),* 1–16.

Hanson, D. M. (2011). *Administrative support of special education teachers.* Northern Michigan University. (Master's Thesis). Retrieved from www.umu.edu.

Horrison-Collier, A. (2013). *Special education teacher retention: The relationship between mentoring, job satisfaction and the retention of special education teachers.* (Doctoral Dissertation). Retrieved from http://digitalcommons.georgiasothern.edu.

Kaff, M. F. (2004). Multitasking is multitaxing: Why special educators are leaving the field. *Preventing School Failure, 48(2),* 10–17.

Katsiyannis, A., Zhang, D., and Conroy, M. (2003). Availability of special education teachers: Trends and issues. *Remedial and Special Education, 24,* 246–53.

Littrell, P., Billingsley, B., and Cross, L. (1994). The effects of principal support on special and general educators' stress, job satisfaction, school commitment, health, and intent to stay in teaching. *Remedial and Special Education, 15(5),* 297–310.

Maslach, C., and Jackson, S. (1984). Burnout in organizational settings. *Applied Social Psychology, 5,* 133–53.

Morvant, M., Gersten, R., Gillman, J., Keating, T., and Blake, G. (1995). *Attrition/retention of urban special education teachers: Multi-faceted research and strategic action planning. Final Performance Report,* Volume 1 (No. ERIC Document ERIC Reproduction Service No. ED338154) Eugene, OR.

Nagel, L., and Brown, S. (2003). The ABCs of managing teacher stress. *The Clearing House, (76)5,* 255–58.

Nelson, J. R., Maculan, A., Roberts, M. L., and Ohlund, B. J. (2001). Sources of occupational stress for teachers of students with emotional and behavioral disorders. *Journal of Emotional and Behavioral Disorders 9(2),* 123–30.

Prather-Jones, B. (2011). How school administrators influence the retention of teachers of students with emotional and behavioral disorders. *The Clearing House, 84,* 1–8.

Pullis, M. (1992). An analysis of the occupational stress of teachers of the behaviorally disordered: Sources, effects, and strategies for coping. *Behavioral Disorders, 17(3),* 191–201.

Retish, P. (1986). Burnout and stress among special educators and others. *B.C. Journal of Special Education, 10(3),* 267–70.

Roach, A. (2009). Teacher burnout: Special education versus regular education. *Marshall University.* (Thesis). Retrieved from http://mds.marshall.edu/etd/810/.

Schlichte, J., Yssel, N., and Merbler, J. (2005). Pathways to burnout: Case studies in teacher isolation and alienation. *Preventing School Failure, 50,* 35–40.

Singh, K., and Billingsley, B. S. (1996). Intent to stay in teaching: Teachers of students with emotional disorders versus other special educators. *Remedial and Special Education, 17,* 37–47.

Stiver, R. L. (1982). *Factors affecting attrition of teachers of the emotionally disturbed: Training and employment considerations.* Oshkosh: University of Wisconsin.

Sutcher, L., Darling-Hammond, L., and Carver-Thomas, D. (2016). *A coming crisis in teaching? Teacher supply, demand, and shortages in the U.S.* Pala Alto, CA: Learning Policy Institute.

Sweeney, D. P. and Townley, A. J. (1993). Stress among general and special education teachers of students with emotional or behavioral disorders: Possible implications for full inclusion. In R. B. Rutherterford, Jr., and S. R. Mathur (Eds.), *Monograph in Behavioral Disorders: Severe Behavior Disorders of Children and Youth, 16,* 102–10.

Texas Center for Educational Research (2006). *Texas study of personnel needs in special education.* Executive summary. Austin, TX: Texas Center for Educational Research (http://www.tcer.org).

U.S. Department of Education Office of Special Education Programs, Study of Personnel Needs in Special Education (2000). *A high-quality teacher for every classroom. Spense fact sheet* (http://www.copsse.org).

Van Acker, R. (2009). *You don't know Jack: How do we prepare teachers to address needs of students with emotional and behavioral disorders.* Paper presented at the Teacher Educators for Children with Behavioral Disorders Conference, Tempe, AZ. Retrieved from http://TECBD. Asu.edu/2010/You_don't_know_jack!:pdf.

Westervelt, E. (2016, September 15). Frustration. Attrition. Burnout: It's time to address the national teacher shortage. *NPR ED: How Learning Happens.* Retrieved from http://www.npr.org/sections/ed/2016/09/15/493808213/frustration-burnout-attrition-its-time-to-address-the-national-teacher-shortage.

Westling, D. L., and Whitten, T. M. (1996). Rural special education teachers' plan to continue or leave their teaching positions. *Exceptional Children, 62(2),* 319–35.

Wisniewski, L., and Gargiulo, R. M. (1997). Occupational stress and burnout among special educators: A review of the literature. *The Journal of Special Education, 31(3),* 325–46.

Wrobel, G. (1993). Preventing school failures for teachers: Training for a lifelong career in EBD. *Preventing school failure, 37(2),* 16–20.

Zabel, R. H., Boomer, L. W., and King, T. R. (1984). A model of stress and burnout among teachers of behaviorally disordered students. *Behavior Disorders, 9,* 215–21.

Zabel, R. H. and Zabel, K. M. (1982). Factors in burnout among teachers of exceptional children. *Exceptional Children, 49,* 261–63.

CONCLUSION

Effective teachers are life savers for many of our students who enter their classrooms. In 2018, teachers have lost their lives saving their students. Brave teachers have advocated and protected their students from harm. The nation applauds those educators and all those who every day, without really knowing it, save their students' lives through their dedication and skillful teaching. Educators are in the noble profession of making a difference in the lives of their children.

From an explanation of the students who are in our classrooms to evaluations to a determination of what services students need, teachers play an integral part in those decisions. Effective teachers build positive relationships with students. A key question asked, in the shootings occurring in 2018, is whether they would have occurred if the students would have had a positive relationship with an adult who could have reached them before they took such devastating action.

One of the most critical aspects of programs for students with emotional/behavioral disorders (E/BD) is organizing the physical space of the classroom. Understanding where to put the student's desks, learning centers, and staff desks. Effectively organizing the physical space of a classroom increases academic achievement and reduces disruptive behavior. Other critical areas of programs for students with E/BD include: explaining behavioral expectations of the classroom to the students and developing effective procedures for reintegrating students with E/BD into regular education classrooms.

Most adults agree that relationships affect children and youth's welfare. Teachers who build positive relationships with students confirm students' emotional experiences and promote a sense of security and belonging that supports their active engagement. A positive relationship with a supportive adult can shield children and youth from trauma and other negative life experiences and can provide the personalized responsiveness and scaffolding necessary for adaptive skill building in the face of disruptive or challenging life events

When working with students with E/BD challenges, it is critical that teachers work together with parents, other educators within the school building, and agencies outside the school. The chapter on collaboration set out to provide the skills needed to collaborate for success.

The last chapter of Volume 1 has focused on taking care of ourselves. If we lose sight of how important it is that we manage our stress and have a healthy lifestyle, we cannot work effectively with our students.

APPENDIX A

When the FBA *should* be conducted	When the FBA *must* be conducted
• When any student's problem behavior impedes his/her learning or the learning of others. 	• When a student's problem behavior impedes his/her learning or the learning of others. • When suspensions exceed 10 days or amount to a change in placement. • When a student is placed in an interim AES for 45 days when his/her misconduct involves weapons or drugs. • When a due process hearing officer places a student in an interim AES for behavior that may cause bodily injury.

IDEA 2004 and Proactive Measures for Conducting FBAs and BIPs

APPENDIX B

Content Overview of the FAI

Topic	Sample Question
Description of behavior	What is the behavior, topography, frequency, and duration of the behaviors?
Setting events that predict or set the occasion and nonoccurrence of challenging behavior	What medical or physical conditions does the individual experience (ADHD, seizures, asthma, tics)?
Antecedent events that predict the occurrence or nonoccurrence of the challenging behavior	When (i.e., time of day) are the behaviors most and least likely to occur?
Consequences that maintain behavior	What are the specific consequences or outcomes the student gets when the behaviors occur in various situations?
Efficiency of the challenging behavior	How rapidly does the behavior result in consequences or outcomes?
Functional alternatives	What socially appropriate behaviors or skills does the student know already?
Existing forms of communication	How does the individual typically communicate (e.g., complex speech, signs/gestures, communication boards, electronic devices)?
Communicating or working with the student	What things can you do to increase the likelihood that a teaching session or activity will go well with the student?
Reinforcer inventory	What types of edibles, toys and objects, activities at home, school, and community does the individual enjoy?

History of interventions   What has been attempted to decrease or
                                              eliminate the challenging behavior?

APPENDIX C

Key Components of Effective E/BD Programs

Component 1: A requirement that prior to a student being referred for eligibility as E/BD, a comprehensive functional assessment has been conducted and an associated BIP has been developed and implemented with integrity (Hanover Research, 2012; Jones et al., 2004; Jones, 1987; Jones, 1998).

Component 2: A positive, supportive staff models effective communication skills in their interactions with colleagues and students (Jones et al., 2004; Neel et al., 2003; Reitz, 1994; Yell et al., 2013).

Component 3: Consistent use of effective classroom management methods (Jones et al., 2004; Reitz, 1994; Yell et al., 2013).

Component 4: A general behavior-management program that provides uniform structure, high expectations, and clarity regarding students' progress toward their behavioral goals (Hanover Research, 2012; Jones et al., 2004; Neel et al., 2003; Reitz, 1994; Yell et al., 2013).

Component 5: A comprehensive cognitive-behavior management and social skills program that includes helping students describe and evaluate their behavior and develop alternative strategies (Jones et al., 2004; Neel et al., 2003; Reitz, 1994; Yell et al., 2013).

Component 6: Staff needs to implement meaningful and developmentally appropriate instructional practices (Jones et al., 2004; Neel et al., 2003; Reitz, 1994; Yell et al., 2013).

Component 7: An individualized behavior management program is developed for each student (Jones et al., 2004; Neel et al., 2003; Yell et al., 2013).

Component 8: An ongoing process of providing students with interpretive interventions directed at helping them understand the dynamics of their behavior problems (Jones et al., 2004).

Component 9: The use of data-based decision-making (Jones et al., 2004; Neel et al., 2003; Yell et al., 2013).

Component 10: A systematic reintegration process (Callahan et al., 1993; Jones et al., 2004; Reitz, 1994).

Component 11: A program offering assistance to parents and guardians (Jones et al., 2004; Neel et al., 2003; Reitz, 1994).

Component 12: A plan for coordinating community resources to support students and their families (Jones et al., 2004; Reitz, 1994).

Component 13: Frequent opportunities for students to practice and use newly learned skills (Hanover Research, 2012; Neel et al., 2003; Yell et al., 2013).

Component 14: Provisions for ensuring that the skills and behaviors learned in the treatment setting will be transferred to school, family, neighborhood, and work environments (Neel et al., 2003; Reitz, 1994).

Component 15: Opportunities when appropriate to work with peers (Neel et al., 2003; Reitz, 1994; Yell et al., 2013).

Component 16: Commitment to sustained intervention for children and adolescents who require long-term support and care (Neel et al., 2003).

Component 17: Appropriate physical space and organization that minimizes disruptive behavior and facilitates effective instruction (Guardino and Fullerton, 2010; Neel et al., 2003; Yell et al., 2013).

APPENDIX D

Fundamentals for organizing the physical space in your classroom

- Permit orderly movement.
- Keep distractions to a minimum.
- Make efficient use of available space.
- Organize classroom space so that the students can attend to the teacher (Evertson and Emmer, 2009).

Keys to making sound decisions regarding the classroom environment

- High-traffic areas should be free of congestion.
- Staff must be able to observe all students at all times.
- Materials that are frequently used by staff and students should be readily available.
- Students' seating arrangements should allow them to see lessons without moving their desks (Evertson and Emmer, 2009).

Designing the physical environment

- Arrange furniture (student and teacher desks, bookcases, tables, computers, plants, aquarium).
- Arrange room dividers.
- Decorate wall space to create a pleasant environment.

- Provide areas for personal space (Guardino and Fullerton, 2010).
- Clear pathways between individual versus group activity areas (Visser, 2001; Weinstein, 1979).
- Make a clear distinction between individual versus group activity areas (Guardino and Fullerton, 2010).
- Organize areas by adding shelves, labels, or cubbies (Evans and Lovell, 1979; Weinstein, 1979).
- Arrange student seating facing away from visual distractions such as doorways and windows (Guardino and Fullerton, 2010).
- Alter classroom to ensure a clear line of sight (Guardino and Fullerton, 2010).
- When determining student seating, teachers should implement a flexible approach to seating arrangements to accommodate the various learning functions that occur in the classroom.

Setting up classroom seating arrangements

- Keeping all students in the staff's sight to maximize supervision (Savage and Savage, 2010).
- Staff must be in close proximity to the students (Savage and Savage, 2010).
- Potentially problematic students should be seated next to students who exhibit appropriate behavior (Smith and Yell, 2013).
- When determining student seating, teachers should implement a flexible approach to seating arrangements to accommodate the various learning functions that occur in the classroom (Smith and Yell, 2013).
- Use tables for small group instruction (Yell et al., 2013).
- Desks should not be facing sources of distraction (e.g., windows, doorways) (Yell et al., 2013).
- Separate students' desks far enough apart in order not to encourage inappropriate student exchanges.

APPENDIX E

Guidelines for Reintegration of Students with E/BD

Step 1. Long-Range Planning and Preparation

1. Planning for reintegration and establishing exit criteria should begin during the Individual Education Plan (IEP) process. At all initial staffing meetings:

   - Identify skills the incoming student will need for success in less restrictive settings, including (a) behavioral, (b) social, and (c) academic skills.
   - Develop long-term goals on the IEP based on skills needed in future less-restrictive settings.
   - Develop and communicate exit-criteria for staffing out of the E/BD classroom.
   - Implement behavioral, social, and academic classroom interventions that (a) focus on integrated classroom expectations, and (b) promote generalization of skills to the integrated setting.

2. Implement a systematic classroom behavior management system that trains for generalization (e.g., through the use of level system-thinning reinforcement schedules, changing expectations in different levels).

3. Collect and maintain ongoing data on each student's behavioral, social, and academic progress.
4. At all subsequent IEP reviews, focus on progress toward expectations of the integrated setting and update IEP goals and objectives (e.g., determine progress made toward long-term reintegration goals, determine present levels of readiness for reintegration).

Step 2. Immediate Preparation for Reintegration

1. After determining a student's readiness for reintegration, notify all persons who will be involved in the reintegration program (e.g., the student, parents, regular education teacher, and administrators) of impending reintegration plans and procedures.
2. Assess several prospective reintegration settings. Meet with regular education teacher and conduct thorough systematic classroom inventories of:

    - Teacher expectations, including behavioral, social, and academic expectations.
    - Classroom routines and procedures.
    - Assignment completion expectations.
    - Attendance and make-up work policies.
    - Grading policies.
    - Test-taking expectations.
    - Homework policies (see Appendices F, G, and H for classroom inventory assessments).

3. Match the student's behavioral, social, and academic characteristics to the most appropriate reintegration setting and teacher:

    - Choose and notify the prospective teacher of possible reintegration.
    - Schedule a meeting with the teacher to discuss the reintegration program.

4. Prepare the receiving teacher during a one-on-one meeting:

- Discuss the purpose(s) of reintegration and secure the teacher's willingness to collaborate throughout the process.
- Discuss the readiness of the student for initial reintegration (e.g., characteristics, strengths, weaknesses).
- Discuss support to be provided to the receiving teacher, including (a) initial assistance (e.g., daily contact/communication, immediate classroom assistance, problem-solving assistance, crisis intervention), (b) follow-up and evaluation procedures, and (c) contingency plans in the event of unexpected problems (e.g., student becomes uncooperative or noncompliant).

5. Prepare the student during a one-on-one meeting:

- Discuss expectations and policies of the reintegration setting, and any modifications to the current special education program which will take place.
- Discuss a timeline for beginning reintegration.

6. Modify expectations, routines, and policies in the special education class to more closely approximate those in the reintegration setting:

- Modify the reinforcement schedule to match those in the regular education environment.
- Modify instruction and curriculum materials to match those in the regular education environment.

7. Continue to document the student's readiness for reintegration into the prospective setting. Keep data on:

- The student's adherence to any modified expectations, routines, and policies within the special education classroom.
- The student's behavioral and social performance while using any modified reinforcement schedule/procedures while in the special education classroom.

- The student's academic performance while using any modified curriculum materials.

Step 3. Initiating Reintegration

1. Prior to beginning reintegration, introduce the student to the receiving teacher. In this meeting, the following should be done:

    - Review the expectations, routines, and policies of the setting.
    - Review initial assistance to be provided to the receiving teacher.
    - Review follow-up and evaluation procedures.
    - Review continued expectations for the student within the special education classroom.
    - Review contingency plans in the event that (a) problems arise in the reintegration setting, and (b) problems arise in the regular education settings.

2. Begin reintegration with one class, period, or subject. Add classes systematically. Consistent success in the first class must be evident before adding another class.

Step 4. Follow-Up and Evaluation

1. Maintain daily communication with the receiving teacher initially, using either personal contacts or a written reintegration monitoring sheet (see Appendix I).
2. Collect and maintain data on the student's functioning in the reintegration setting, including:

    - Accuracy and completeness of academic assignments.
    - Homework completion.
    - Behavioral and social performance.
    - Performance of all mainstream expectations, routines, and policies.

3. Continue to collect and maintain data on the student's behavioral, social, and academic performance in the special education classroom.

4. Conduct periodic meetings with all persons involved in the reintegration program to:

- Review overall performance in the reintegration setting.
- Review performance in the special education setting.
- Consider modifications in the student's reintegration program including increases or decreases in the amount of reintegration time.

APPENDIX F

Reintegration Course Description Checklist

Subject: Grade: Teacher:

Textbook Title/Author: Reading Level:

General goal of course:

Best time to contact you:

Information Input *(Instructional Methods)*   **Information Output** *(Types of Assignments)*

Information Sources   Assessment Format

Information Sources	Assessment Format
_____ Textbook	_____ Short Answer
_____ Worksheets	_____ Essay
_____ Lecture	_____ Multiple Choice
_____ Discussion	_____ True/False
_____ AV Material	_____ Matching
_____ Audio Tape	_____ Computation
_____ Hands-On Experience	_____ Math Word Problems
_____ Observation	_____ Oral
_____ Internet	_____ Performance
Other _____	_____ Portfolio
	_____ Fill-in-the-blank, with or without Word Bank
	_____ Criteria-Based Assessment
	Other _____

Structure   Assignments

      _____ Directed   _____ Reading

_____ Independent

_____ Peer Tutor

_____ 1-on-1 Adult

_____ Small Group

_____ Large Group

Other _____

_____ Worksheets

_____ Short Papers

_____ Term Paper

_____ Demo/Lab Projects

_____ Art, Media Projects

_____ Oral Reports

_____ Group Discussion

_____ Computation

_____ Math Work Problems

_____ Maps, Charts, Graphs

Other _____

Academic Skills Needed

_____ Becoming Interested/ Motivated

_____ Getting Started

_____ Paying Attention to the Spoken Word

_____ Paying Attention to the Printed Word

_____ Following Directions

_____ Keeping Track Materials, Assignments

_____ Staying On-Task

_____ Completing Tasks on Time

_____ Working Independently

_____ Learning by Listening

_____ Expressing Him/Herself Verbally

_____ Reading Textbooks

_____ Reading Study Sheets or Tests

_____ Understanding What Is Read

_____ Writing Legibly

_____ Expressing Him/Herself in Writing

_____ Spelling

Behavior Skills Needed

_____ Getting Started

_____ Coming to Class on Time

_____ Coming to Class Prepared

_____ Following Directions

_____ Staying in Seat

_____ Staying On-Task

_____ Completing Tasks on Time

_____ Working in Groups

_____ Working Independently

_____ Participating in Class Discussion

_____ Understands/Follows Safety Rules

_____ Asks Questions or for Help When Needed

_____ Being Cooperative

_____ Being Attentive

_____ Accepts Help When Given

_____ Accepting Responsibility for Own Actions

_____ Seeing Relationships

_____ Remembering

_____ Drawing Conclusions/
Sharing Inferences

_____ Understanding Cause and
Effect; Anticipating Consequences

Other Academic Skills Needed   Other Behavior Skills Needed

_____ Note Taking

_____ Outlining

_____ Punctuation

_____ Writing Sentences

_____ Writing Paragraphs

_____ Dictionary Use

_____ Independent Research
(Library / Internet)

_____ Measuring

_____ Manual Dexterity

_____ Math Skills

Other Prerequisites   Grading Criteria

Homework Policy   Extra Credit

Make-Up Work Policy   Additional Comments

Please attach: Syllabus, Grade Contracts, Rubrics, etc.

APPENDIX G

Reintegration Student Checklist

Student:	Disability:	Date:
School:	Grade:	Case Manager:
Basic Achievement Reading Level:	Source:	Date:
Math Level:	Source:	Date:

Support Needed from Special Education Staff? ☐ Extensive ☐ Moderate ☐ Occasional

IEP Goals:

Students' Likes (interests and hobbies):

Students' Dislikes:

Is the home amenable to helping with student's program? ☐ Yes ☐ No

Please indicate on each of the items: Strength (+)   Weakness (-)   Cannot Do (cross out item)

Information Input *(How Student Learns)*

Information Output *(How Student Responds)*

Information Sources

_____ Textbook

_____ Worksheets

_____ Lecture

_____ Discussion

_____ AV Material

_____ Audio Tape

_____ Hands-On Experience

_____ Observation

_____ Internet

Other _____

Assessment Format

_____ Short Answer

_____ Essay

_____ Multiple Choice

_____ True/False

_____ Matching

_____ Computation

_____ Math Word Problems

_____ Oral

_____ Performance

_____ Portfolio

_____ Fill-in-the-blank, with or without Word Bank

_____ Criteria-Based Assessment

Other _____

Structure

_____ Directed

_____ Independent

_____ Peer Tutor

_____ 1-on-1 Adult

_____ Small Group

_____ Large Group

Other _____

Assignments

_____ Reading

_____ Worksheets

_____ Short Papers

_____ Term Papers

_____ Demo/Lab Projects

_____ Art, Media Projects

_____ Oral Reports

_____ Group Discussion

_____ Computation

_____ Math Word Problems

_____ Maps, Charts, Graphs

Other _____

Learning Problems

_____ Becoming Interested/ Motivated

_____ Getting Started

Behavior Problems

_____ Getting Started

_____ Coming to Class on Time

_____ Paying Attention to the Spoken Word

_____ Paying Attention to the Printed Word

_____ Following Directions

_____ Keeping Track of Materials, Assignments

_____ Staying On-Task

_____ Completing Tasks on Time

_____ Working Independently

_____ Learning by Listening

_____ Expressing Him/Herself Verbally

_____ Reading Textbooks

_____ Reading Study Sheets or Tests

_____ Understanding What Is Read

_____ Writing Legibly

_____ Expressing Him/Herself in Writing

_____ Spelling

_____ Seeing Relationships

_____ Remembering

_____ Drawing Conclusions/ Sharing Inferences

_____ Understanding Cause and Effect; Anticipating Consequences

_____ Coming to Class Prepared

_____ Following Directions

_____ Staying in Seat

_____ Staying On-Task

_____ Completing Tasks on Time

_____ Working in Groups

_____ Working Independently

_____ Participating in Class Discussion

_____ Understands/Follows Safety Rules

_____ Asks Questions or for Help When Needed

_____ Being Cooperative

_____ Being Attentive

_____ Accepts Help When Given

_____ Accepting Responsibility for Own Actions

Other Academic Skills Needed

_____ Note Taking

_____ Outlining

_____ Punctuation

_____ Writing Sentences

_____ Writing Paragraphs

_____ Dictionary Use

_____ Independent Research (Library / Internet)

Other Behavior Skills Needed

_____ Measuring

_____ Manual Dexterity

_____ Math Skills

Comments and Suggestions

APPENDIX H

Reintegration/Inclusion Student Inventory/Course Description Comparisons

Student Inventory	Course Description

Student Inventory

Course Description

Information Input *(How Student Learns)*

Information Input *(Instructional Methods)*

_____ Textbook

_____ Worksheets

_____ Lecture

_____ Discussion

_____ AV Material

_____ Audio Tape

_____ Hands-On Experience

_____ Observation

_____ Internet

Other _____

_____ Textbook

_____ Worksheets

_____ Lecture

_____ Discussion

_____ AV Material

_____ Audio Tape

_____ Hands-On Experience

_____ Observation

_____ Internet

Other _____

Structure

_____ Directed

_____ Independent

_____ Peer Tutor

_____ 1-on-1 Adult

_____ Small Group

_____ Large Group

Other _____

Structure

_____ Directed

_____ Independent

_____ Peer Tutor

_____ 1-on-1 Adult

_____ Small Group

_____ Large Group

Other _____

Student Inventory—Learning Problems

Course Description—Academic Skills Needed

_____ Becoming Interested/ Motivated

_____ Getting Started

_____ Paying Attention to the Spoken Word

_____ Paying Attention to the Printed Word

_____ Following Directions

_____ Keeping Track of Materials, Assignments

_____ Staying On-Task

_____ Completing Tasks on Time

_____ Working Independently

_____ Learning by Listening

_____ Expressing Him/Herself Verbally

_____ Reading Textbooks

_____ Reading Study Sheets or Tests

_____ Understanding What Is Read

_____ Writing Legibly

_____ Expressing Him/Herself in Writing

_____ Spelling

_____ Seeing Relationships

_____ Remembering

_____ Drawing Conclusions/ Sharing Inferences

_____ Understanding Cause and Effect; Anticipating Consequences

<u>Student Inventory—Behavior Problems</u>

_____ Getting Started

_____ Coming to Class on Time

_____ Coming to Class Prepared

_____ Following Directions

_____ Staying in Seat

_____ Staying On-Task

_____ Becoming Interested/ Motivated

_____ Getting Started

_____ Paying Attention to the Spoken Word

_____ Paying Attention to the Printed Word

_____ Following Directions

_____ Keeping Track of Materials, Assignments

_____ Staying On-Task

_____ Completing Tasks on Time

_____ Working Independently

_____ Learning by Listening

_____ Expressing Him/Herself Verbally

_____ Reading Textbooks

_____ Reading Study Sheets or Tests

_____ Understanding What Is Read

_____ Writing Legibly

_____ Expressing Him/Herself in Writing

_____ Spelling

_____ Seeing Relationships

_____ Remembering

_____ Drawing Conclusions/ Sharing Inferences

_____ Understanding Cause and Effect; Anticipating Consequences

<u>Course Description—Behavior Skills Needed</u>

_____ Getting Started

_____ Coming to Class on Time

_____ Coming to Class Prepared

_____ Following Directions

_____ Staying in Seat

_____ Staying On-Task

_____ Completing Tasks on Time

_____ Working in Groups

_____ Working Independently

_____ Participating in Class Discussion

_____ Understands/Follows Safety Rules

_____ Asks Questions or for Help When Needed

_____ Being Cooperative

_____ Being Attentive

_____ Accepts Help When Given

_____ Accepting Responsibility for Own Actions

_____ Completing Tasks on Time

_____ Working in Groups

_____ Working Independently

_____ Participating in Class Discussion

_____ Understands/Follows Safety Rules

_____ Asks Questions or for Help When Needed

_____ Being Cooperative

_____ Being Attentive

_____ Accepts Help When Given

_____ Accepting Responsibility for Own Actions

APPENDIX I

Inclusion/Integration Slip

Name   **Class**   **Date**

- Was on-time to class
- Demonstrated appropriate behavior
- Used appropriate language
- Followed all directions
- Completed all work

Comments:

Signature

APPENDIX J

Special Education Attrition Research

Attrition Factors	Primary Findings	Author(s) and Year
Experience	Teachers with less experience are more likely to leave than their experienced peers.	(Billingsley and Cross, 1992; Miller, Brownell, and Smith 1999; Singh and Billingsley, 1996)
Induction	Special educators reporting less effective mentoring are more likely to indicate intent to leave the field.	(Whitaker, 2000)
School climate	Special education teachers reporting poor school climate are less likely to stay in the field than those who report positive school climates.	(Billingsley, 2004; Dillon, 2007; Miller et al., 1999)
Administrative support	Inadequate administrative support is linked to more role problems, less job satisfaction, increased stress, lower levels of commitment, and fewer professional development opportunities: lack of administrative support is a central reason given by special education teachers for leaving the field.	(Billingsley, 1993; Billingsley et al., 1995; Cancio et al., 2013; Cancio et al., 2014; Cross & Billingsley, 1994; George et al., 1995; Gersten et al., 2001; Morvant, 1995; Nelson et al., 2001; Singh and Billingsley, 1996; Westling and Whitten, 1996)
Colleague support	Special education teachers reporting lower levels of colleague support are more likely to leave the field than	(Gersten et al., 2001; Miller et al., 1999; Morvant et al., 1995)

Attrition Factors	Primary Findings	Author(s) and Year
	those experiencing greater level of support: lack of colleague support is associated to decisions to leave the field.	
Professional development	Special education teachers reporting less professional development support were less likely to remain in teaching.	(Gersten et al., 2001)
Teacher roles	Issues with teacher overload, conflict, ambiguity, and manageability are related with attrition, excessive paperwork, meetings, and lack of time for teaching are contributors to decisions to leave the field.	(Billingsley et al., 1993; Billingsley et al., 1995; Cross and Billingsley, 1994; Gersten et al., 2001; Morvant et al., 1995; Singh and Billingsley, 1996; Westling and Whitten, 1996)
Caseloads	Greater caseload contributes to attrition; high numbers on caseload and inappropriate placement of students with disabilities contributes to attrition.	(Billingsley et al., 1993; Billingsley et al., 1995; Morvant et al., 1995; Schnorr, 1995)
Isolation	Problems with isolation, feeling misunderstood, and not being valued by principals and colleagues leads to attrition.	(Billingsley et al., 1993; George et al., 1995; Morvant et al., 1995)
Service-delivery	Teachers of students with E/BD are most likely to leave; teachers in secondary schools are more likely to leave than those in elementary schools.	(Billingsley, 1993; Pullis, 1993; Singer, 1992; Singh and Billingsley, 1996; Wisniewski and Gargiulo, 1997)
Resources	Inadequate resources contribute to attrition.	(Billingsley, 1993; Billingsley et al., 1995; Morvant et al., 1995)
Decreased feelings of accomplishment	Feeling an inability to deal with crisis situations.	(Cross and Billingsley; 1994; Gersten et al., 2001; Miller et al., 1999; Singh and Billingsley, 1996)
Job satisfaction	Special educators who are dissatisfied with their jobs are more likely to leave their positions.	(Brownell, Smith, McNellis, and Miller, 1997; Cross and Billingsley, 1994; Gersten et al., 2001; Singh and Billingsley, 1996)

Attrition Factors	Primary Findings	Author(s) and Year
Commitment	Special education teachers with lower levels of commitment are more likely to leave their positions.	(Cross and Billingsley, 1994; Gersten et al., 2001; Miller et al., 1999)

APPENDIX K

Positive and Negative Reasons to Stay in the Field

Positive factors associated with
intent to stay in the field

- Opportunities for training in technology and other professional development
- Support for disciplinary problems
- Administrative support for teacher ownership of the classroom
- Access to curricula
- Principal awareness, care, understanding, and availability
- Support system of paraprofessionals and general education colleagues
- Adequate physical space
- Assistance with paperwork

Negative factors associated with
intent to leave the field

- Lack of awareness and understanding of students with EBD and their programming needs
- Lack of current, appropriate textbooks and materials
- No time for paperwork
- No access to resource services
- A perceived administrative attitude that does not support the inclusion of students with EBD
- Resistance to acknowledgment of mental health disorders
- Inappropriate disciplinary actions

APPENDIX L

Categories and Strategies for Reducing Stress and Burnout

Category	Suggestions
Develop a positive and adaptive frame of mind by ...	Eating right, relaxing, being active, maintaining interests outside of school, setting realistic expectations, maintaining hope, looking at the positives, reflecting on one's work, and making work as enjoyable as possible
Form positive collegial relationships by ...	Using effective communication skills, connecting with positive people, getting involved in social activities, supporting others
Use effective organizational strategies by ...	Chunking large projects, prioritizing tasks, evaluating existing organizational systems, delegating responsibilities, enlisting student support, using data for multiple needs
Embrace change, innovation, and new opportunities by ...	Remaining current in the field, conducting research, connecting with local and state entities, setting professional goals
Collaborate with administrators by ...	Keeping administrators informed, sharing positives, thanking administrators for their support, focusing on student needs
Assess one's stress and burnout level by ...	Completing checklists and rating scales, noting changes in energy, passion, or interests, talking to others

Adapted from Cancio & Conderman (2007).

APPENDIX M

Checklist of Strategies for Reducing Stress and Burnout

#	Strategy	Yes	No	If No, Plan of Action
	Developing A Positive Frame of Mind: Do I . . .			
1.	Set reasonable expectations?	☐	☐	
2.	Leave work at work?	☐	☐	
3.	Maintain a balance between my professional and personal life?	☐	☐	
4.	Look for the positives in a situation?	☐	☐	
5.	Focus energies on what I can change or have control over?	☐	☐	
	Forming Positive Collegial Relationships: Do I . . .			
6.	Practice effective listening skills (e.g., reflective listening)?	☐	☐	
7.	Participate in social activities outside of work with colleagues?	☐	☐	

#	Strategy	Yes	No	If No, Plan of Action
8.	Provide assistance to colleagues when they need assistance?	☐	☐	
	Organizational Strategies: Do I . . .			
9.	Prioritize tasks in order of importance (e.g., charting, IEPs)	☐	☐	
10.	Separate large projects into small steps (e.g., annual reviews)	☐	☐	
11.	Use self-management strategies with students?	☐	☐	
12.	Delegate appropriate tasks to your paraprofessional?	☐	☐	
	Embracing Change, Innovation, and New Opportunities: Have I . . .			
13.	Volunteered as a mentor in my building?	☐	☐	
14.	Made connections with special education colleagues in other districts?	☐	☐	
15.	Conducted action-based research?	☐	☐	
	Collaborating with Administrators: Do I . . .			
16.	Keep my administrator informed about what is going on in my classroom?	☐	☐	
17.	Focus more on solutions rather than challenges?	☐	☐	

#	Strategy	Yes	No	If No, Plan of Action
18.	Communicate to colleagues and administrators that "it is all about the kids"?	☐	☐	
	Assessing Level of Stress: Have I . . .			
19.	Assessed whether or not I have symptoms of stress and burnout?	☐	☐	
20.	Developed positive coping strategies to alleviate stress and burnout?	☐	☐	
21.	Developed a plan to revitalize myself?	☐	☐	

Adapted from Cancio and Conderman (2007).

ABOUT THE AUTHORS

Edward Cancio is currently an associate professor at the University of Toledo in Ohio. Ed has a wealth of experience in working with students with challenging behaviors in schools in Illinois. He holds a doctorate from Utah State University and is the past president of the Ohio Council for Children with Behavioral Disorders. He is a recognized speaker in the area of teacher stress and implementing motivational systems for students.

Mary Camp has over forty years of experience in working with students with behavioral and emotional disorders. She was the administrator of a special school for students with severe emotional disabilities in Peoria, Illinois. Mary holds an ED.D. from Illinois State University. She is a past president of the Illinois Council for Children with Behavioral Disorders. She is a recognized speaker in the area of autism, transition, and evidence-based interventions. She has frequently taught college classes as an adjunct professor at various colleges.

Beverley H. Johns is currently a professional fellow at MacMurray College in Jacksonville, Illinois, and has had over thirty-three years' experience working with students with the most significant behavioral disorders. She was the administrator of an alternative school for students with behavioral disorders. She is the author or co-author of twenty-two books on the subject of working with students with special needs. She is a past president of the Council for Children with Behavioral Disorders and serves on the board of the Illinois Council for Children with Behavioral Disorders.